Between Two Cultures

Between Two Cultures

The Life of an American-Mexican
as told to
JOHN J. POGGIE, JR.

The University of Arizona Press
Tucson   Arizona

About the Author . . .

JOHN J. POGGIE, JR., has concentrated his anthropological studies
in the areas of sociocultural change and Latin America. The story
of Ramón is one of the publications which resulted from his fieldwork in the central highlands of Mexico in 1966–67. A number of
journal articles and a chapter in the book *Technology and Social
Change* (edited by Bernard and Pelto) point up other effects
of economic and technical modernization on Mexican rural social
and cultural life. Author Poggie is also joint editor with Robert N.
Lynch of the volume *Rethinking Modernization: Anthropological
Perspectives.* He holds a Ph.D. in anthropology from the University of Minnesota and has taught at the University of New Bruns-
wick, Canada. He joined the staff of the Department of Sociology
and Anthropology at the University of Rhode Island in 1969.

Second printing 1975

THE UNIVERSITY OF ARIZONA PRESS

I. S. B. N.-0-8165-0334-6
L. C. No. 72-84765

To Erika, Jonathan, and Kristina

Contents

Introduction

RAMÓN GONZALES* is a man who is part of two very different cultures — American and Mexican. This is his autobiography. Although Ramón was born in Mexico, his parents brought him to the United States as an infant, and he grew up in the United States where he lived until he was in his early forties. However, he never acquired United States citizenship. Ramón was twenty-one years old the first time he was deported to Mexico. In the next two decades of his life he was deported many more times but he always reentered the United States illegally. Ramón repeatedly "jumped the border" into the United States because, as he said, "I didn't feel at home in Mexico." Eventually, after increasing difficulties with the law, Ramón decided to try to live in Mexico permanently.

Thus it was only after that decision that Ramón lived in Mexico with the intention of remaining indefinitely. When Ramón arrived in Mexico to stay he was culturally more American than Mexican, and he was called *El Pocho* by the Mexicans because he was "different" — his speech was different and his behavior was different.

Ramón appears to have adjusted reasonably well to living in Mexico, and he does not appear to be embittered by his frustrating experiences on both sides of the border. On the one hand he has become more "Mexican" in some of his ideas and in his speech, but on the other hand he probably never will feel fully Mexican because of the impact of his many years in the United States. He probably

---

*Pseudonyms have been used in this volume when actual names of persons or places would intrude on the privacy of individuals.

always will prefer baseball, hamburgers, milkshakes, and fishing to bullfights, tamales, and pulque.

I first met Ramón in 1967 in the central highlands of Mexico while I was doing anthropological fieldwork on cultural change in the area. He was selling arts and crafts in a tourist shop, something he was very good at due to his fluent and idiomatic English and his friendly, good-humored sales style. Ramón worked for me part-time for several months doing interviews in the communities in the area, and I came to know him well during this period. I liked Ramón because he was very easy-going and relaxed. He often told humorous stories to me while we drove from place to place doing the interviews. He seemed to take things as they came without much show of emotion. The only times Ramón displayed strong feelings to me were after we began recording his life story, when he told me about the loss of his mother, and, to a lesser degree, when he talked about the girl he loved a great many years ago in California. Otherwise he could be characterized as being emotionally "flat." His strategy for handling conflict situations was to avoid or deny them. Many episodes in his life that he related to me ended with the words "so I took off."

Ramón was a slim, dark-haired, fairly good-looking man of about medium height. His complexion was moderately dark. He usually wore a sport shirt, trousers, and a gray cardigan sweater which had one button missing. In his dress two items set him apart from the majority in his village: he never wore a sombrero, and he frequently wore sunglasses.

Ramón enjoyed working for me because it gave him a chance to talk to a North American about his life in the States. We talked a great deal about California and his life there — and how different life now was in Mexico. He lived with his new, very young bride in a small, two-room rock house. The outside of the house was decorated with small stones pushed into the mortar, which is a pre-Columbian technique in central Mexico. The front of his house was also decorated, in typical Mexican fashion, with many plants hung up in tin cans.

The house was furnished with a bed, a wardrobe, a table and chairs, and a kerosene stove. Several of these items he was paying for on time. There was no water, no bathroom, no outhouse. A public water faucet was in the process of being installed on his street. Ramón's wife raised a few turkeys and a pig in their yard, and on cool nights the young chicks shared the warmth of the house. Tall cactus plants formed a fence around the yard. Many times when I came to pick up Ramón he would be warming himself in the morning sun outside his house, as there was no heating in the house, and temperatures often dropped to the freezing point during the night in winter.

Ramón's town consisted of less than a thousand people and was mainly a peasant community where the growing of corn and beans predominated as the main economic activity. Because of its proximity to Teotihuacán, a major archaeological site visited by many tourists, about fifteen to twenty people from the town were employed as wage-earning salesmen like Ramón at one of the several tourist shops in the area.

The region around the town is dry and brown most of the year, but during the summer months there is sufficient rain for growing crops. The most prominent features of the landscape are the prickly pear cacti and maguey plants. The town itself has a paved road into it from the main highway, but the streets in town are unpaved.

*   *   *

At first in our discussions of his life in the States, Ramón talked about the furniture, television sets, clothes, cars, and other material comforts he had enjoyed. Gradually the other aspects of his life began to unfold. We agreed that it would be worthwhile to present his life in the form of an autobiographical book. Thus he spent many hours relating the events of his life into a tape recorder, a method brought to attention by Oscar Lewis. The recording sessions were held over a two-week period in daily blocks of two to three hours. Most of the sessions were carried out inside my field vehicle because it was a quiet and comfortable place to sit. When it got too hot inside the car we would sit down in a shady spot outside and continue. At first I asked a number of questions to keep the flow of material going as well as to clarify certain points, but later this was no longer necessary. At times Ramón would continue dictating even when I was absent from the car. One time early in the interviewing, when I was playing back the tapes in the evening, I was rather taken aback to hear an account of his prison term at San Quentin, an episode he had elected to relate when I was absent from the car. After this incident he talked freely about his difficulties with the law.

It was with this bank of taped material that I was able to put together the life history of Ramón, from his birth in Pueblo Nuevo, a small settlement near Irapuato, Guanajuato, to my chance meeting with him some forty-five years later. This book represents about eighty percent of the unedited tapes. Only redundant or repetitious materials have been deleted. The major part of the editing task was arranging the material in roughly chronological order and pulling together the pieces that fit together, since Ramón often would return to a previously mentioned event and enlarge upon it. Except for elimination of some of the "you knows," with which Ramón often began and ended sentences, and occasional clarification of phrasing, the narrative remains essentially in Ramón's own words.

*   *   *

The kind of social and cultural environment that Ramón has had to cope with is a very complex one. Not only did he grow up as part of a minority group in the United States, but he later had to adjust to living in a culture which in many ways was foreign to him. Indicative of his cultural conflict is the fact that on the one hand he rejects native curers as nothing more than superstition ("they just take your money"), but on the other hand he believes that he was twice cured by one, once from a limp resulting from burns and once from an intestinal problem.

Ramón's life was made even more difficult by the fact that he grew up without a mother and in poverty. Thus his behavior involves many of the factors that characterize others in these situations. Difficulty in loving relationships and difficulties with the law are two of the most evident characteristics to be seen in Ramón's behavior.

The story of *El Pocho* is in some respects atypical for people of Mexican heritage who live in the southwestern United States. Ramón is not part of the Chicano movement that has gained so much momentum since the late 1960s. Although *El Pocho* grew up in Chicano-land, his struggle for his rightful place in the world was being carried out in Mexico rather than in the southwestern United States. This, of course, is related to the fact that he is an American-Mexican rather than a Mexican-American; that is, he is a national of Mexico who is culturally more American than Mexican.

In other respects Ramón is not so atypical in that he is part of a larger class of people who are the American-Mexicans on both sides of the border. It is difficult to estimate how many such people there are, but there certainly are a substantial number of Mexican nationals-whose lives have been affected to varying degrees by exposure to American culture. We know much less about these people than we do about Mexican-Americans.

In yet another sense Ramón is characteristic of a larger class of humans all over the world: people who feel that they do not belong solidly to one cultural group. These are the world's marginal men. It is true that some marginal men use their position of existing between two or more cultures to certain advantage, frequently as cultural "brokers" or intermediaries. Ramón, for example, is a cultural broker in his role as a salesman to tourists. However, the research of anthropologists and sociologists has shown that being marginal is generally a difficult position with which to cope. The ethnic enclaves in our urban areas as well as "over-Americanized" recent immigrants are examples of ways in which people have tried to work out problems of marginality. Marginality can come from emigrating to a new cultural setting, but it also can result when individuals are denied meaningful roles in a culture. Thus many minority power movements and the countercultures that have sprung up in the United States and elsewhere can in certain respects be thought of as groups of marginal men seeking places for themselves in the world. It would seem that all humans need to belong to a cultural group that is meaningful to them. If they do not feel that they belong to such a group, they will seek such a group for themselves. It is in this sense that Ramón is no different from other marginal men throughout the world.

Ramón's autobiography is the story of one person's search for a place in the world. I hope, as did Ramón in relating to me his life story, that this personal document will enable others to know what it is to be one kind of marginal man.

Acknowledgments

The fieldwork grant which enabled me to gather these materials in 1966–67 was supplied by the National Institute of General Medical Sciences (Grant No. GM 001164) through the auspices of the

Department of Anthropology, University of Minnesota, E. Adamson Hoebel, chairman.

I wish to thank Professors Frank C. Miller and Pertti J. Pelto for scholarly counsel related to my fieldwork in central Mexico. Nancy Hansen transcribed my original tapes into an unedited manuscript. Erika R. Poggie spent many hours helping me type and edit the manuscript. The staff of the University of Arizona Press, and particularly Karen Thure, offered skill and cooperation in projecting the manuscript into book form.

I especially wish to acknowledge the great confidence and trust that Ramón Gonzales had in me and in my efforts to help him relate his life story. I feel fortunate to have had the opportunity to learn about the life of an American-Mexican in so personal a way.

JOHN J. POGGIE, JR.

Between Two Cultures
Map

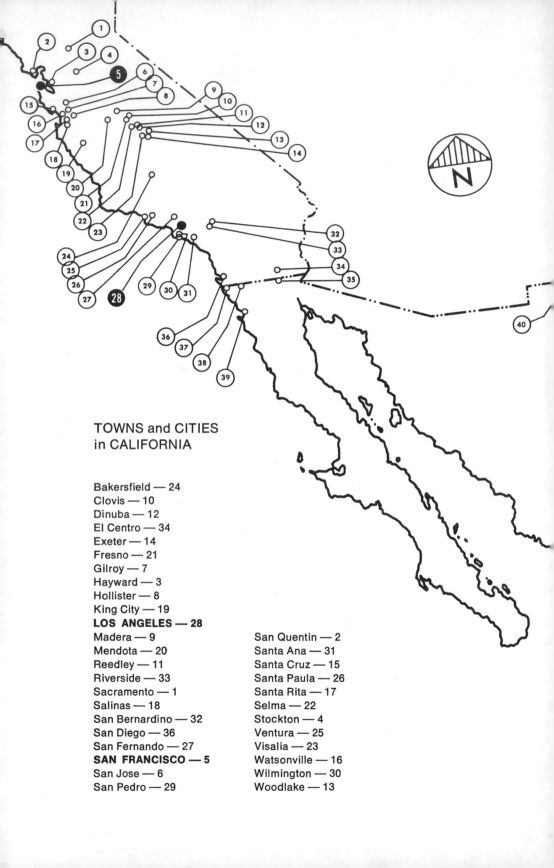

TOWNS and CITIES in CALIFORNIA

Bakersfield — 24
Clovis — 10
Dinuba — 12
El Centro — 34
Exeter — 14
Fresno — 21
Gilroy — 7
Hayward — 3
Hollister — 8
King City — 19
LOS ANGELES — 28
Madera — 9
Mendota — 20
Reedley — 11
Riverside — 33
Sacramento — 1
Salinas — 18
San Bernardino — 32
San Diego — 36
San Fernando — 27
SAN FRANCISCO — 5
San Jose — 6
San Pedro — 29

San Quentin — 2
Santa Ana — 31
Santa Cruz — 15
Santa Paula — 26
Santa Rita — 17
Selma — 22
Stockton — 4
Ventura — 25
Visalia — 23
Watsonville — 16
Wilmington — 30
Woodlake — 13

TOWNS and CITIES in MEXICO

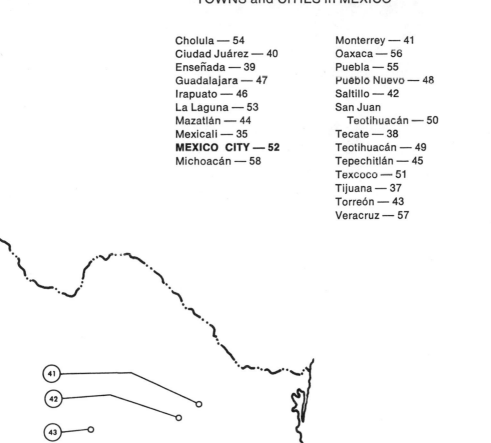

Cholula — 54
Ciudad Juárez — 40
Enseñada — 39
Guadalajara — 47
Irapuato — 46
La Laguna — 53
Mazatlán — 44
Mexicali — 35
MEXICO CITY — 52
Michoacán — 58

Monterrey — 41
Oaxaca — 56
Puebla — 55
Pueblo Nuevo — 48
Saltillo — 42
San Juan
  Teotihuacán — 50
Tecate — 38
Teotihuacán — 49
Tepechitlán — 45
Texcoco — 51
Tijuana — 37
Torreón — 43
Veracruz — 57

JOE TIBBETS

1. Introducing *El Pocho*

THEY CALL ME *El Pocho** in my town because I live all my life in the States, and because at first when I came here to Mexico I didn't know how to speak very good Spanish. All the words that I used to speak I used to make. . . . Like for *push,* I used to say *"púshale,"* you know. That's not a Spanish word. In Spanish you say *"empújale."* But that's the way the pochos talk. They couldn't understand me here, so that's why they call me that.

Well, Pocho is my name. They nicknamed me El Pocho here in Mexico. I didn't have no trouble learning Spanish. Every time I heard somebody talk, I used to listen how they talk, you know, and right away I think, well, that word doesn't go that way. This friend of mine, Eduardo Lopal, he's a policeman in Mexico City. I used to help him in English, and he used to help me in Spanish. And he still says, "No, the word goes this way." He also used to work in the shop where I work, the Tienda Azteca. It took me about six months to learn how they speak Spanish here.

In the States we used to speak half English and half Spanish, you know. In Spanish if you want to say, "Let's go uptown" you say, *"Vamos al centro."* In pocho talk you say, *"Vamos al tango."* That's the way the pochos talk in California. Like another example, like they say *pantalones* for pants here in Mexico. In California a lot of the young guys, they don't call them *pantalones.* They call them *trabuchos.* And like *realist* is shirt. Here in Mexico it's *camisa.*

---

* The word *pocho* is used in Mexico as a pejorative term denoting one who is culturally prejudiced toward the United States, or one who has returned from the United States with little memory of Mexican language and culture.

[1]

Different words. Just like in the United States . . . like they have a different way of talking in New York; even English in New York they talk a different way. You don't understand them when you hear them talk. Pocho talk is slang, *calo,* that's what they call it. Like they say *mi gina,* my girlfriend. *Mi huisa* is a girl who likes to fool around and have relations with a lot of guys. She's a girl that's no good.

Well, I came here near Teotihuacán, near these pyramids, a year ago, you know. One day I went traveling with a guy, and we went to a place next to San Juan, a little town named La Laguna. They had a little store there where they sell beer. And we were drinking there, me, him, and his cousin. Then three guys from the pyramids came there. One guy, they call him *El Burro,* and another guy, I forget the other guy's name. But a short guy, you know, we call him *Chaparro.* In English we would call him Shorty.

So he came there and then he said, "So you're El Pocho." And I says, "Yeah, I'm El Pocho." And he says, "Do you think you're too good?" I says, "Why do you say that?" He says, "Because there are a lot of people that say you speak English." "That doesn't mean that I'm too good," I told him. "Well, to me it seems you think you're better than me. I speak English too." I told him, "I might speak better English than you, but that doesn't mean that I'm better than you. It's just that I know how to speak English better." So he said, "Come outside here!" And I told him, "I don't want to hit you because I know you people here don't know how to fight," and all that. So I hit him, you know. I hit him about two times and I knocked him out.

Now I go by the pyramids and he sees me and he don't talk to me. But I never let him get too close. I stay away from him, you know. He just knew a few words of English. Those guys sell souvenirs at the pyramids. They just speak a little English to sell to the tourists. So he got mad, because once I went to sell statues at the pyramids. That's why he was mad. Because I could talk better to the tourists so I sold more than he did. That's why I don't like to go around the pyramids or sell like that, because right away there's envy, you know. Because I speak better English than they do.

What I miss most about the States . . . over there you have a nice job, you know . . . maybe it's not yours when you rent a house, but you have everything that is necessary in your house, like you have your television, stove, and everything. Because in the States a house is all full of furniture, you know. Over there you can have a nice job, and you work good. That's what I miss. Like here I can't have nice furniture like you do in the States. It's not easy, because here the pay is too low. And you can't furnish a house in one year or two years, like that, because it takes a lot of money. It takes a long time before you can furnish a house. A nice comfortable house, a nice place to live in — that's what I miss most.

Because in the States you live a different life than here. When I was in the States, over there, I always was dressed good. Over there you can buy yourself three, four pairs of shoes, like that, and here it is not easy to buy them. Because the pay is maybe fifteen pesos a day, a little more than a dollar, and a suit costs you five hundred pesos. Twelve and a half pesos make a dollar, so that's forty dollars for a suit — not everybody makes forty dollars.

When I was in the States, I never did miss anything from Mexico. When I was in the States, I never did like to come to Mexico, you know. Because I was raised in the States. I lived all my life in the States. I never got to think of coming to visit Mexico or anything like that.

When they put me over the border, right away I would come back because I would never get used to Mexico. So as soon as the Immigration put me on this side, I wait only for one hour or two hours, like that. And then pretty soon I start looking up places where I could cross the border. And then I would cross and wait for a bus to pass, you know. I never thought the Immigration would pick me up. I just thought I'd go back, jump over the border. I jumped the border all total about nine times. And so many times they put me across, you know.

Finally I said, "I think I'll try to see if I can stay in Mexico." So I tried one time, you know, coming over here. I tried to stay here, for three months I stayed here. Finally I decided, "Ah, I'll go back to the United States." Because I was not used to the kind of life that the people lead here in Mexico.

Because, you know, it's hot in California, but after work you come home and take a shower, and then you dress up and go out. Maybe to a movie, or maybe to a drive-in, or maybe you go to a recreation hall, like the YMCA. You practice lifting weights or boxing or tennis, or play cards. Or you can play checkers or dominoes or chess. I used to go to the YMCA for recreation, play there, pass the time. They don't have that around here.

I haven't gone fishing since I left California. I'm done with fishing. In the States I used to do a lot of fishing. I would like to go, but it takes money to buy the fishing rod and all that. And then, here you have to go by car, and I have no car to go fishing. It's a long distance. You have to go maybe to Acapulco and go up in the mountains someplace where they have fishing. Like Mazatlán is a good point to go fishing, Mazatlán. It's a long ways from here to Mazatlán. In the States you work five days and a half, and then you have to go and get ready for Sunday. You make your plans where you are going to go. And here, the only place you go here is to the movies. Only to the movies.

We have time, but, I mean, here it is not as easy to go to those places like in the States. Over there, say you have a friend, you can ask him, "What are you going to do tomorrow?" He says, "Well, I have nothing in mind." You tell him, "Well, let's go fishing." You know, plan to do something. So he says, "How about going hunting, deer hunting?" Up in Watsonville we used to go deer hunting.

It's not because I have a wife. I still could go. In North America there would be places nearby where I could go and pass a Sunday or weekends, stuff like that. Maybe it's because I know so many people in the States, and here I don't know as many people. Here they don't do nothing. They don't go away like that. The only place they go is to Mexico City. That's the only place they invite me to go. Like I see somebody and they say, "Well, let's go to Mexico City to the movies." That's the only place they invite me.

The boys that I used to work with in the Tienda Azteca, they used to tell me, "Well, let's go to see this movie. It's a good one." And we would go to the movies. And that's the only thing we'd go to. The only place we go to here is to Chapultepec Park, in Mexico City. Lots of tourists there. They have boats, you get in and row, you know. That's the only place that I've been to. With my wife and her parents we went. Me, her, and my half sister, we all got in the boat. And then we never know how to row, and I got them all wet! They'd get all angry because I'd get them wet!

That's how come I used to come back and forth, because I didn't feel at home in Mexico, even though I was born here. To me, I felt that the States was my home because I lived there most of the time.

And I know so many people in the States. Like here in Mexico I don't know very many people. Most of the people that I know are in the States. I know almost every town in California. I know the people, you know. There are families that I know. I stop in any town and they see me and know me. And here I go to any town and they don't know me. They don't know me because I never lived here.

Even now I feel like I would be more at home in the States. Even now that I have been away for, say, five years. When I go back, you know, right away a lady that knows me says, "Where have you been?" Or she says, "Oh, you've been in jail." These ladies were very well acquainted with my father; they were really friendly. I used to go back when they hadn't seen me for four or five years, and they would ask me, "Where have you been? Have you been in jail?" And I would tell them, "No, I have been in Mexico." And they would say, "Oh, we thought you were in jail or something." I still send Christmas cards to certain people in the States.

The foods I like here in Mexico are like fried beans, fried potatoes, fried eggs, like that. Bread with butter. In the States, in the mornings I used to like toast with jelly, or hot cakes with coffee, waffles, or cornflakes. Then for dinner I used to eat like pork chops or fried chicken, with a soup, like chicken noodle soup. I used to like that very much. I like lamb chops, pork chops, tuna fish. Fried fish. Then hot dogs, hamburgers, cheeseburgers. I love those.

Here in Mexico they don't make them like they do in the States. Every time I go to Mexico City I see hamburgers, they call them *hamburguesas*. But, you know, they don't even taste like the hamburgers they make in the States. That's why I don't buy them. That's why I buy a *torta*. A torta is like a sandwich; they put ham, they put tomato, they put onions.

Over there I used to eat nothing but hamburgers, hot dogs, cheeseburgers, jumbo. A jumbo is a hamburger with a double layer. With hot dogs we used to buy french fries, and then coffee or a chocolate milkshake. I used to love it, to go to a restaurant like that. Sometimes we used to go, two, three boys, and invite two, maybe three girls, and then we used to go to this drive-in place. And you park and then a girl comes and asks you what you want, and then you order. I would order a cheeseburger, maybe a couple of cheeseburgers or hamburgers with french fries and coffee. I like ketchup with the hamburgers.

I used to like hamburger steak, you know. In the United States I used to go to a restaurant, and every time I went to this restaurant the lady knew right away what I was going to ask for. She used to say, "Oh, don't tell me — hamburger steak!" I used to say, "Oh you!" Because I used to laugh. Hamburger steak, you know, with a lot of ketchup. I used to love to go there. I used to go eat in that restaurant all the time. That place they give you good pork chops too. I used to drink only coffee and chocolate milkshakes.

I used to eat tortillas in the States. But tortillas in the States are different than the ones from here. The tortillas in the States are made out of flour, and here in Mexico they are made out of corn. So it's a different kind of tortillas. But see, in the Mexican restaurants over there, you can go and they have enchiladas, they have tacos, fried eggs, refried beans, just like here. They make a soup out of beef — you just put the beef in the pan, and then you put cabbage, carrots, rice, like that.

I like American food better than Mexican food. Even here, when I get a chance I eat American food. I told my wife to make like spaghetti, spaghetti with cheese, and steaks. Not just regular steaks — you get a steak and you press a lot of bread until it's just a powder, and then you fry it like that, and they come kind of brown on top. Yeah, breaded steak.

I haven't planned it yet, to go back. I would like to go back, just for a visit. I would like to go visit, to visit my relatives and friends, for maybe thirty days, and then I could return. And then if I decided that I could stay over there, then I would try to stay. But, I mean, jumping the border, I don't like to jump the border no more.

See, jumping the border, somebody picks you up and you probably go before a judge, and he has to sentence you for a certain time, say six months, one year, or eighteen months in the "facilities," they call it, where they have nothing but wetbacks. The last time I had to go before a judge, he gave me eighteen months of suspended sentence. Eighteen months suspended sentence with five years probation. That means that right now I could go back, but then, you see, the probation is over. But anyway, I would go before the judge. If I got caught I would go before a judge, and he would probably sentence me to hard labor, two years or eighteen months. That's why I don't like to go back.

A lot of times I stayed quite awhile waiting to be deported. One time I waited six months before/I was deported. I never tried to get papers. It's just that a lot of people used to jump. At that time, thousands used to jump. The Immigration at that time didn't amount to much because the war was on. They needed people to work, so they didn't never watch the borders too close. Until the war was over, that's when they started getting tough. Then they really started getting tough.

I'm getting to be forty-five years now, not too old, but I don't like to cross the border no more. I got tired of it. It is better to work here and live. I used to do it, maybe because I didn't have a wife. Now I have a wife and decided to settle down. Sometimes I think about going back, or maybe going just to the border and get a permit to cross the border. I never tried to get papers. It just happened that it was so easy to cross that you didn't think of it, the papers. But maybe one of these days I will try to get some papers legally and cross the border.

That way you won't be afraid like when I was in the States illegally. When you would be in a city, right away when you see a cop, you think he is going to come and ask a question or so. Or when I was driving a car, in the mirror I used to look behind me and when I used to see a cop in back of me, right away I felt he was going to stop me or something. When I saw any Immigration that I would pass on the way, oh, I would go fast in the car, get them lost, you know.

I've been a few years here in Mexico now, working, and you don't have to be afraid of a cop in back of you. Because you don't have to be afraid of anything. You live here and you work. You don't make as much money as in the States, but you can live more happy here. In them days when I used to cross the border I used to make a lot of money, but still you didn't live a good life. You know, you don't even sleep good. You don't dare sleep good because right away you have to be awake in case you hear a noise of the Immigration coming in. Because they used to come at night. They used to come at night when everybody would be asleep. Pick you up. So sometimes I didn't even stay in a house. I used to stay out in the fields, take a blanket and sleep out in the fields. Here you don't feel like that. You can rest good, you work, you finish, you don't have to be afraid of somebody running after you. In the States you dress good, you buy your clothes, you have good meals and everything, but you are not free. Here you are free! I used to run back and forth before I had a wife. Then I said, "I am going to get married. Maybe if I get married I won't cross the border."

And sometimes I tell my wife, "I am going back to the States." She says, "You stay here. Oh no, you are not going." She says she wants me to stay here and be with her. But I talk. I tell her when I go to the border I will take her with me, just to the border. Maybe there I can get a better job than here. Even if I went to Mexicali or Tijuana I would stay in the tourist business. Because Tijuana is known as a tourist town; thousands of tourists cross every day and there are thousands of little shops for tourists that sell things. I would probably like to live in Tijuana, because in Tijuana it's very close to Mexicali, and then Tijuana's not hot. Just a climate like say here, by the pyramids. This is a good climate here. This kind of climate you would have in Tijuana. The ocean is very close. And then there's this town named Enseñada, where you can go fishing or something on weekends.

2. Early Experiences and Family Life

My name is Ramón Gonzales. I was born in Pueblo Nuevo, Guanajuato, on August 31, 1922. My father's name is Nazario Gonzales and my mother's name is Candelaria Gonzales. I have three brothers: one is David Gonzales, another is Jaime Gonzales, and another one is Edward Gonzales. I have two sisters, Alicia Gonzales and Guadalupe Gonzales. Except for David they are all half brothers and half sisters. Two real brothers died before I was born. One was named Ramón like me, he died about a year before I was born. Ramón died of typhoid. They got a *curandero* for him — this was in Pueblo Nuevo. The curanderos do a lot of things like cure you with eggs — they put eggs on your body and all that. It didn't help him, so he died from that. In them days there were no doctors, you know. It must have been 1921, a year before I was born.

I was born in the house where my parents lived. It was a town of maybe three, four thousand. It was an adobe house, with five rooms. My father worked taking care of the sheep, goats, and cattle. They were my grandfather's cattle. My father was a shepherd, and he milked the cows and goats. My grandfather was one of the richest men there in Pueblo Nuevo at that time. He had five sons and two daughters. He had an adobe house; it had four rooms and a little kitchen, and then in the back it had a big corral where they used to keep the cows and cattle, and that's where my father used to milk the cows. And on one side they used to have a lot of plants, you know. Plants like roses, daisies, sunflowers, and some other kinds of flowers, I don't remember the names. But for something to eat, my grandfather, father, and uncle used to farm. They farmed corn and cumin, spices, barley, chick-peas, frijoles, peanuts, watermelons, cantaloupe. They sold all of it. In Irapuato there's a big market where you sell it.

They say that my mother was very religious then. She used to go to church every day, about five o'clock in the morning. My father was not too religious; he just used to go once in a while because he used to go very early in the morning to take the sheep and the goats and the cattle out to the pasture. Then about two o'clock they used to bring them in, and he put them in their places and then he had to milk them. He would milk every cow and every goat.

We had a shrine there, not actually a shrine, like a picture, you know, of the Virgin of Candelaria, which is the Virgin of our town. See, every second of February they celebrate a big fiesta in our town which begins on January the twenty-sixth up til February the second. February second is a holiday when they take the Virgin out and they take it to all the nearby towns, to all the little ranches they take it, and there were a lot of firecrackers, and they carried it to all those towns so they could see the Virgin.

I remember this because when I was about twenty-one years old I was deported and I came back to my town. I stayed there for about six months with my grandfather and my father. My grandfather got me a job there driving a truck, driving from Pueblo Nuevo to Irapuato hauling corn to the mills. My grandfather and grandmother still lived in the same house, the one I was born in.

*   *   *

I heard the story then of how my father wanted to move to the States years ago. See, my father borrowed some money to go to the States, from a friend. Not a friend, a relative — this man was married to my father's sister, and he loaned my father some money to go to the States. But he was telling my father not to go because my father had a beautiful wife, and he would lose his wife in the States. But my father wanted to go anyway, and so he borrowed the money, and he took my mother and me through El Paso. And from El Paso we went clear to California. You didn't need to have any papers or anything, you just pay. At the border there was a bridge there and they just paid five centavos.

I was about six months old. They went clear to Mendota, California. They just happened to go there because a friend, he was there before, and he came and told them about California, and then my father went back with him, see. They went to Mendota because that is in the San Joaquin Valley, and that is known for cotton-picking. Mendota is a big cotton place.

I heard that at first when we got there it was pretty hard because, you know, the wages in the States. . . . Maybe you've heard that they didn't pay enough money, they paid ten cents an hour in them days when I was small. They used to give just a little wage, so we had kind of a hard time. And then my mother used to have like a boarding-house, so they could get money. They got a house like out in a lot of fields. The ranchers have a lot of houses for all the workers, you know, so in there she got a big place like a boardinghouse, but only for meals, not to sleep. My mother used to cook the meals for these men, Mexican workers. They worked out in the fields picking cotton. That's how they used to get by, you know. In Mendota they lived about six years.

The house where I lived was a small house just like a little room, a little kitchen, you know, and it had water inside. It was a wood house — all the houses in California are wood. We used to live out on a ranch, not in the city of Mendota. From Mendota to this little ranch was about two miles. The population of Mendota was then maybe eight thousand. I didn't go to school there.

We moved from Mendota to San Bernardino when I was about six years old. All my relatives lived in San Bernardino, that's how come we moved. Like a cousin of mine named Susanna, my mother's niece. She was born in Mexico but moved there, and they are still living there. And I have some other relatives on my father's side, like Vicente López. He has a lot of sons and daughters who still live there in San Bernardino, see. My relatives wrote to my father and told him to move to San Bernardino because there he could make more money picking oranges than he could on the cotton. So that's how come we moved there.

We moved over there and he picked oranges, and then I used to help him too, you know, on the bottom there picking oranges. I was small but I could pick a little bit and help him. He used to get, I think it was three cents a box. I used to help him on the weekends, and then summers when there was no school, vacation from school, I used to help him every day.

The first day of school my cousin took me, she must have been about twenty-one. I was about six or seven years old. That was in the first grade — I didn't go to kindergarten. The name of that San Bernardino school was Ramona School. I remember that first day when I went to school, she took me to the principal there, Mr. Harris I think it was, and they took me to a teacher named Mrs. Thorn. I still can remember her name because she was very nice to me, because I think that I was the only one that was from Mexico. There were Mexican kids but they were all from the city, born in the States. I was the only one that was born in Mexico.

The teacher was very nice, and she introduced me to all the students. Pretty soon they all started talking to me in Spanish. I didn't know any English at all; I went there to learn English. And they were very helpful, you know, try to teach me. Because when we used to go out to play I used to go out and sit by myself, see, because I wasn't very acquainted with all the boys. Pretty soon one boy told me, "Come on, let's go play." He's the one that every time I go back to the States I go visit him — his name was Jesús Valdez, but his nickname was Quityeo. So this Quityeo, he introduced me to all the other boys. Pretty soon we used to go out and play baseball, at school. It took about two months before I got to know them real good, to be playing with them. I was scared because I figured, you know, you're by yourself and they, you know, bunch on you.

Like one time when I was small, one boy told the other guy to pick a fight on me. You know how they put a little stick on your shoulder and knock it off? So they put that on me and told the boy to knock it off. Before he could knock it off I hit him. I hit the boy and they took me down to the principal, and the principal told me not to be fighting and all that. That was in 1928, I think, the first year that I went to school.

One time a bunch of guys beat up on me and then, well, I didn't say nothing that they beat me up, but I said one of these days I'll get even with them. My cousin asked me, "Why did you let them do that to you?" I says, "Oh, I let them do it but one of these days I'll get even. Let it go. One of these days I'll get even." But I never got even, because, how you say, I didn't hold no grudge against them. After that I got very friendly with them and then they told me they were very sorry that they beat me up.

They had an alley there and after school we used to go out

there and fight over a new girl, or . . . you know how kids are. Everybody fought. Sometimes it was, "Why don't you go and fight with this boy in an alley?" I don't like to fight, but, if you don't fight you are a chicken. So I said OK. So we went out there and then when I was fighting with this boy, the brother of this boy wanted to fight with me. So then I said, "No, I don't want to fight you." They were two, you know, and I was only one. Then the father came over and told us that was enough.

We fought with fists, because in the town there was a prize-fighter named José Gonzales, and he used to teach the boys with boxing gloves. He trained little boys. You know how little boys would go with boxing gloves, and fight with other schools. That's how he used to train us. And we knew how to fight.

In grammar school the boys used to form little gangs, and we used to fight. A gang of Mexican boys used to fight with other gangs of Mexican boys. Then a long time ago they used to fight with bicycle chains. You know, the chain on a bicycle? Well, they used to take it off and use it as a weapon, one gang against another one. I never done it because always the captain of the gang is the one that fights with it, with the captain of the other gang. I never was captain. When you get into bicycle chains, a lot of the guys get hurt and some get killed. And then they send you to prison. There are a few guys that I know who got in those fights and are in San Quentin right now, because they killed somebody.

The school I went to was a public school. And the teacher, Mrs. Thorn, got to liking us very much, all the boys, you know. She was teacher for grades one, two, and three. She had a big house and we used to go to her house and she had a lot of trees, like plum trees, orange trees, peach trees, apricot trees. And we used to go there and pick the plums there, cut the grass, and help her clean her yard and everything. She used to give us fifty cents.

We never used to go straight to school. We used to play marbles all the way to school. Sometimes we'd be late and we'd hear the bell, and then we'd stop playing marbles and run. We'd just get in there and Mrs. Thorn would pull our ears, because we were coming in late. And then she used to tell us, "Put your hands out," and she would hit every one of the hands. Or she would make us stand in the corner, just stand in the corner and not turn our heads to the class. Then we used to turn around and be sticking out our tongues at the girls and all that. She used to get mad. I remember one time she was sitting down, and she put me under her desk. "Around here you can't be making no fun at the girls like that." And we all started laughing.

And then I remember one time my friend Quityeo thought of something to do to the teacher. We went and got some thumbtacks, and we put them on her chair so that when the teacher came she would sit down on the thumbtacks. So she sat down on a thumbtack, and she jumped. And she don't want to say anything, she don't want the class to know. So then she caught all three of us. "All you three don't go to recess. I want to talk to you." She took us to the principal.

And you know for punishment the principal. . . . They used to make you bend down and used to hit you with a rubber hose. They hit us three times. Then Quityeo said, "Tomorrow we make the teacher real mad. You wear about four pants, so when they hit us it won't hurt." I said O.K.

So the next day we wear a lot of pants, you know, and then we make the teacher mad and then she take us to the principal. And then she said, "When the principal hits you, just as soon as he hits you once, you all start crying so he won't hit you no more." But instead of me crying, I started laughing because it didn't hurt. And finally he got so mad he hit me and hit me, but it didn't hurt me. So finally he said, "Oh, you get out of here. I'm not going to hit you. I'm going to make you work." Then he used to make us work, cut the grass, work on the ground around the flowers. He used to make us work hard, so finally we decided not to do that to make the teacher mad no more.

We used to make the teacher mad, you know, but she was nice to us. On Saturdays, she used to tell us, "I want you boys to come to my house. I'm going to make a dinner." And all three of us, we used to go to her house. And then she used to make a good dinner for us, and after that was finished, she used to give us money for the movies. She was very nice.

We used to keep on doing things to her, but I mean, even though we did a lot of things to her, she wasn't mad at us. She was nice to us. But after a while I told the boys, "You know the teacher was very nice to us. Let's not make her mad no more." You know, when she was in an accident in her car and her legs broke or something, we all cried like she was our mother. And we went to the hospital and we used to visit her regular.

After a few years in San Bernardino we went back to Mendota

and worked in the same ranch where we used to work, in the cotton. My father wanted to go back, and then we worked irrigating the cotton. We had stayed in San Bernardino for over two years.

My brother was born in Mendota after we went back. I was about eight years old. He was born in the house. In them days they used to have midwives, *parteras* they called them. The doctors couldn't come to the house and take care of the mother. As far as I can remember my mother was nice, you know, but right after my brother was born, she took off. When she took off my brother must have been about three months old. My mother took off and left her baby with my father. She took off and ran away with another man. A Mexican, from Mexico. And he took her and they came here to Mexico.

And then my father had a hard time taking care of my brother. He had to feed him and everything just like a woman does. With a bottle, you know, feeding milk through a bottle. I helped him. When he was working I had to take care of my little brother. Then pretty soon they come and tell me I had to go to school. You know, in the schools they have a sheriff, or what do they call it, truant officer. He came and told my father I had to go to school. So I went to school, and they had a place there in Mendota where they can take care of babies for a while. A nursery. And that's where we used to leave him for part of the time while my father worked. And then after school I used to get him and take him home.

For a long time we lived that way, my brother David, my father, and myself. My father used to cook for us, he used to do everything like a woman does. He used to wash our clothes, iron our clothes, make our food, everything.

What I remember about my mother is that, see, my father used to work in an orchard. This was in Mendota. And all the men used to come for lunch, you know, to the boardinghouse my mother had. There must have been around fifteen of them. And they all used to come in together, but this one guy used to come in last all the time. He used to come in last and I used to see how good my mother used to feed him, you know, good breakfast and all that. Treat him real good. And I used to see. Pretty soon I start seeing this all the time. I used to get mad. I used to get mad and say, "How come you treat this guy so much better than the other guys?" And my mother didn't say nothing.

So one day, this man take to love . . . I guess . . . I went into the kitchen and then I saw him with my mother. I saw him kissing my mother. And I told her I was going to tell my father. And before I could tell my father they took off. When I saw her with that guy I got real mad and I told her how mean she was with my father and all that. And she said she didn't care. So I went to see my father; he had left for work already. He came home and my mother was not there. Only my little brother was in the house, in a crib. He was there and my mother was not there. She had taken off. My father said, "Well, you've got to take care of your brother now that she's gone." He was really upset; he couldn't find her.

But one day, my father and another guy went to town, to Fresno, to buy groceries and clothes. And my father ran into my mother with this man, and my father, he got mad, you know. But they got into a car and closed the windows and then they took off. That's the last time my father ever saw my mother. Then we used to hear stories that she was around some town, like Madera, like Reedley, she used to hang around there.

She used to treat me nice. My mother and father never hit me. Like a lot of boys, their fathers hit them real bad. I never had that kind of a life where my father would hit me. Like a man that I knew in Woodlake that had four sons, and he used to hit his sons with a stick, real hard. I remember one time that he hit one of his sons in the head and all the blood started coming out of his head. My father never hit me like that.

My mother treated me nice. I liked her before, but then when she did that to my father, oh, I hated her, you know. For years I hated her. Even when I was around thirty-five, I still hated her. I says, "If I ever see her, I'll never talk to her." But then a lot of people used to tell me I should forgive her and talk to her and all that.

She never came, you know. But now I don't think I hate her that much because, if I ever see her, I think I will talk to her. Maybe I wouldn't go and live with her, but I would talk to her. And I would never mention nothing about what she did to my father.

I have a picture of my mother. I have a picture here at home. My aunt gave it to me, a picture album, small, you know. And my father got it from my mother. I have it sitting in the house.

They used to get along very well. That's why a lot of people used to tell my father, "You're too good with your wife. One of these days she is going to leave you." Because my father was very good with her. A lot of people tell me my mother liked to fool around before she went to the States. I heard stories that she liked to fool around, you know. I don't know if they are true or not, but I've heard it from relatives of mine. My mother and another aunt of mine — they were married and still they used to fool around with other men. That's why they used to tell my father not to go to the States, because my mother was going to leave him in the States and go with somebody. Well, my father didn't believe it. He trusted her, so he didn't believe it.

Well, when she took off, my father was really upset. He started to drink. He didn't used to drink, but when my mother took off, he started to drink too much. And I used to tell him, "Don't. Don't drink," because then sometimes he would be all drunk and we had to cook our own meals, you know. He just used to get drunk and then he laid down and went to sleep. The next morning he would get up and go to work. After a while he started forgetting about my mother. It took him maybe three or four years before he finally settled down. That was after we moved back to San Bernardino.

He got another wife — he didn't marry this one, he just lived with her for a while in San Bernardino. This was years later. This woman, she had three daughters, and they all lived there. Her name was Paula. My father, it seems, he couldn't get along with this woman. I think her husband died on this woman. My father didn't get along with her and he got separated. Then the Immigration deported this woman back to Mexico, and then we moved to Mendota again.

After my mother left, well . . . like when you have a mother you run to your mother when you want something, anything, you know. But when my mother left, there's nobody there to run to. My father couldn't do anything. He had to work and everything. He couldn't wash our clothes, so we got our clothes all dirty. The women that used to live there in the same place, sometimes they used to wash our clothes. We used to come and say something and they would give us a bath.

I used to think a lot of times, if I would have had my mother, I would have been a different person. All the years that I used to see boys on Mother's Day, that they bake a big cake for their mothers, that they give a lot of gifts, and sometimes I used to cry. Not cry, only tears, that would roll down my face because I see those boys with their mothers. They were so happy they were in her house.

And me and my brother, we used to think of our mother. My brother never did hate my mother. He probably didn't remember her, but he used to say, "I wish I knew where my mother was and I would go see her," and all that. I used to hate my mother for all the hard times that we passed all those years. It was really rough for my father, like to make food, or wash our clothes. We really had a hard time. That's why a lot of people say that my father got old too fast, because he had to do everything the hard way.

Well, a lot of people, they have their mother, and their mother, when they do some wrong, right away their mother has to shame them out. And like we never had a mother. My father was working. He didn't know what we were doing. And the years we had my mother, my mother would know because she would be home. And she know what we would do. And my father he never knew nothing about it. So we used to get into trouble. Not real trouble, but, you know, fight. You do that, you do this, and nobody knows. But if you have a mother, another lady goes and tells your mother, "Well, your son did this." When you only have a father, your father's never home. All the time he's working so he never takes care of you like your mother does. When something happens, you go tell your mother. With your father it's not the same thing. Your father can't do what a woman does. All the time I thought about it — that if I had a mother, some things would have been a lot different.

Most of my life I used to think about that, and I used to think if I ever see my mother I would tell her how mean she was and what hard years we've had with my father. How he was trying to do the things that a woman does and still he couldn't do them.

The years went by, and we never got to see my mother. For thirty-nine years I haven't seen my mother, and I don't think I would really remember her if I saw her out in the street. Because thirty-nine years is a lot of years, and we change a lot. I think if we were passing on the sidewalk I wouldn't recognize her.

Most of the time when I used to miss my mother was on like birthdays. Like mine, you know, or my brother's. Because I used to go to a lot of boys' birthdays, and their mothers would make a big cake and give them a present. And everybody used to gather and eat ice cream. And then when I was eating ice cream like that, I used to stop eating and then the lady of the party would tell me, "Don't worry about your mother." And all the time they used to tell me, "Don't worry no more about your mother. I will be your mother. You can always come to our house and you're welcome." Because they see me like that and all of a sudden my tears would come out. I would feel sad because I didn't have no mother. And I would tell other boys, because all the time they invite me to their parties, "I don't want to go." And they would ask "Why?" "Every time I go to a party like that, I start crying because I don't have no mother." And they would say, "That's all right. My mother said for me to bring you." And I would go.

But every time I would go to a party . . . even now, sometimes on certain occasions, if I hear somebody mention my mother, I feel like the tears want to come out of my eyes. Because I would like to see her just for once. I would like to see her even if I didn't talk to her. Because I heard that she doesn't want to talk to me because she feels, you know, badly, she feels guilty, and she says that's how come she don't come and look for us. But if they told me, "That's your mother," I think I would go and talk to her even if she felt, you know, guilt at what she did. But at least I would know who was my mother.

A lot of times my brother and I used to argue over that. Like I used to tell him that if I ever see my mother, I would never talk to her and I would tell her off. And my brother would say, "How come you don't forgive her? I would like to see my mother; we should forgive her. You hated my mother ever since she took off, but forgive her now." But now I don't hate her as much as I used to years ago. Because years ago, I used to hate her so much that I thought if I see her I would tell her off. Or maybe more, you know. Tell her a lot of bad things that is not right for me to tell my mother, even after what she did, you know. It's not right for me to tell her things.

Most of the time I used to go to Jesús Valdez's mother. That was the boy we used to call Quityeo. I used to stay there, and I used to sleep there in his house. His mother liked me very much; she was nice to me. She had I think four sons. I used to go there every day from when I must have been around ten until I was around thirty years old. I used to give her presents, like a box of candy on Valentine's Day. She was nice to me, and every time I would go there she was glad to see me, like I was her son. That's why I go there.

Jesús' father, Lorenzo, was a very close friend to our father. That man liked to drink, too. But he used to drink, not to get drunk every day, only once in a while, when he used to invite my father. And then I used to tell him, "Don't give anything to my father or he gets drunk and then I can't take him home." He used to say, "Well, he can sleep here, in the house." So they used to stay there and drink and drink. And I used to get so mad, because my father used to drink. And then he said to me, "Well, you go to sleep." Me and my brother and Quityeo used to go and sleep in Quityeo's room. The next day we get up and wash and then we go to school. Then my father would go to work from there.

*   *   *

I have heard from people that my mother lives in Torreón in the State of Coahuila. I know that I have some half sisters from her. I found out from different people that know my mother. They tell me my mother lives over there, and she is very well off and all that. And then the man that took my mother was killed by another man, but I don't know if my mother has another man now or not. She was good-looking, so maybe she took off with some other man. But I haven't seen her since I was around eight or so. I would like to just see her, even though she left us when I was small. I would still like to see her. I would like to talk to her, even though she left me. She must be around sixty-five, something around there. But even so, I would like to see her, talk with her.

When I have money I plan to go and look her up. It would cost at least about two thousand pesos. We would have to go there to the town and rent a place and ask some people for her. Because I don't know where she is, and that's why it takes around two thousand pesos. I would have to ask certain people, maybe ask a priest, go to the *comandante,* because see, most of the babies are registered in the police station. And I would ask them to look her up. Either there or the church, you know. Because when they baptize the babies they keep a record. It would take maybe one or two months to try to locate her.

The people that know she lives in Torreón are my uncles, my mother's brothers, so they know for sure. They don't visit her themselves. Not even my grandfather who lives in Mexicali knows where my mother is. He's my mother's father, and my mother told him that she would only return when he dies. She's just so mad at him. See, my grandfather got mad because my mother left my father, and my grandfather scolded her and that's why she got mad with him and told him she was going to go away and never come back. She never did come back. My mother took off and left my grandfather. My grandmother was very ill, and she died on account of my mother. See, my grandfather was working and my mother was taking care of my grandmother, and when she took off my grandmother didn't have her medicine at the right time and she died. That's why my mother doesn't show up.

My mother, in a way . . . a lot of people say she was mean, but I don't know. I don't know if all the stories they say of my mother are true or not. Most of the people that I have talked to, friends, you know, say she was mean. They tell me, your mother was this, your mother was that, you know. She took off, though, so she must be mean.

3. Later Childhood

Most of my childhood I spent in San Bernardino. We lived there, my father, my brother, and myself from when I was about nine until I was about fourteen. We lived there, but we didn't have very much in San Bernardino. We just had a small house, and we used to pay, I think it was forty dollars a month. And then we didn't have very much in it, just one bed for me and my brother, and one for my father. We used to have a radio. And then in the kitchen we didn't have no gas stove, like that, we used to have one of those iron stoves; you put wood in it. We had one of those because we were very poor then, and we didn't have no money to buy a gas stove. My father was the only one that worked all the time because we were going to school then.

When I was about nine years old I used to sell newspapers in San Bernardino to help my father because we didn't have no money. We used to sell the *Los Angeles Times* and the *Examiner* on Sundays and Saturdays; the local paper from San Bernardino was the *Herald Express*. I used to make good money, because I had a good corner where I used to stay and sell them all the time. Lots of times we make fifteen dollars a day, or eight, or five. It depends on the papers. Later I stopped selling papers because I started getting older.

Another job I used to do to make money when I was about twelve years old was work in a circus. I used to sell *paletas*. *Paletas* are frozen suckers. *Circo Gutiérrez,* that was the name of the circus. That was in the United States, but the circus was from Mexico. A good circus. In San Bernardino they have a place where they make frozen suckers. We used to get them there and sell them in the circus, and when the circus wasn't there I sold them at the beach, like Balboa

Beach, close to Los Angeles. And then I used to sell the frozen suckers in most of the towns around there, like Riverside.

And then we used to go to this rancher and steal his oranges to sell them. Because in those days they used to pay very little money, it was the depression, you know. I think it was 1931. We used to steal the oranges to sell them. We used to sell one dozen oranges for fifty cents, and that's how we used to go to the movies. When the owner caught us stealing his oranges, he said, "You don't have to steal the oranges, you can come and ask me for them and I will give them to you." After that we used to help him clean around the trees. He used to give us a lot of oranges.

Then I used to sell fruit like cantaloupe and watermelon. I went door to door, knocking on the door, "Would you like to buy a cantaloupe or a watermelon?" Sometimes we used to make good money, selling like that, but lots of times you would be ashamed to knock on the door because there would be girls there. You would be kind of ashamed to be selling fruit like that.

One other thing we used to do to make money was pick grapes. We used to pick red grapes and black grapes and put them on trays. Then the sun would dry them and make raisins. This was still in San Bernardino, when I was about ten or eleven. We got paid one cent a tray. Usually we would pick one hundred trays, so we would get one dollar. Sometimes we picked two hundred trays a day. But now I am a better picker, I could make more than that. But for a young boy one hundred trays is a lot of trays!

*   *   *

The first time I got into trouble with the law I was about nine years old. That was when I used to sell papers in San Bernardino. We were poor, you know; we didn't have no money to buy nothing. My father couldn't buy himself a shirt, nothing. It was really rough. And we didn't have nothing to wear, and we were without shoes. We used to go to school barefoot. My father didn't have no money to buy us shoes. So, we used to sell newspapers outside a big department store, and these boys said, "Well, you've got no clothes, let's go into the store and we'll put some shirts in between the papers." And I says, "No, they'll catch us." "No, they won't catch us," so I says "OK." And we went in. But you know, we were so small we didn't know nothing about how to do those things. We got some shirts and put them in between the newspapers, and this man probably saw us, but he didn't stop us from getting the shirts. Then as soon as we were going to step out of the door, he caught us and told us, "Come on you boys, you're under arrest." He was a store policeman. Then he took us to the detention home, and they told us that we were going to stay there until we were twenty-one years old. And I says, "No!" I was really scared.

But they didn't keep us there. A man there talked to my father, and finally they let us out and said, "Well, next time you do this, I'm really going to put you in jail until you're twenty-one years old." So then I didn't want to get into any more trouble, because I didn't want them to put me in the reformatory until I was twenty-one.

I remember when they were making a movie there in San Bernardino one time. I think Mickey Rooney was making a movie. I was maybe eight or nine years old. I remember that when they finished making the movie, they leave all that wood so that poor people can take it. Well, everybody was taking the wood out, and an uncle* of mine was in there getting a load of good wood.

Some men must have took some beam off, and all of a sudden, when we were under the house helping my uncle, the building started coming down. Then everybody came running out. I remember I ran out, but my uncle couldn't run, and the building, when it came down, it hit him on the back I think, or maybe in the legs. But he didn't get hurt very bad. We had to carry him to his house because he was a little hurt. That's the closest I got to getting covered with wood. I had to run.

I used to help this uncle of mine all the time but he was very cranky. One time he told us, "Well, let's go bring some wood." So we had that wagon full of wood, too heavy for one person to pull. Then he got mad at us for something, so we got mad, and we left him there with that wood, all by himself. And we came home. I was about eight years old.

Another time we went with this uncle, we walked from San Bernardino back clear to the mountains. And there he wants us to go

---

*Ramón addresses all relatives of his parents' generation as aunt and uncle, irrespective of their actual kinship relationship. This is typical usage and is employed in deference to age.

and get some watermelons, to steal the watermelons from the field. We had this little cart that we made, with four wheels, and it was pretty high. And he says, "We're going to get some watermelons from here, and I'm going to take them home." So we got those green watermelons, big ones, you know. We put about twelve watermelons in that cart, and then we had a lot of fun. We broke open watermelons just to get the heart out, and just eat the best part, you know. He always wanted us to go get watermelons.

The owner of these watermelons, he had a shotgun, but he didn't put no bullet, he used to put like wheat, or maybe rock salt. He knew that the people would steal the watermelons. So he would shoot you with this thing, you know, and it hurts! Because another time about five guys, we went out there just to eat watermelons. Well, we're all in a bunch, eating watermelons, when this man comes and we run. And he shot with that thing and hit us in the back. That's how I know it really hurts!

One time this boy, Robert Hernández, and this Quityeo, we went to Fowler's Jewelry Store in San Bernardino. I was about nine years old, I think. We went to look at the rings and watches, and I was going to buy a wristwatch on time. This other boy, while we were looking at stuff, he got one of those gold rings and put it inside an orange, and then he threw the orange outside on the sidewalk. I didn't know he put a gold ring in there and that he threw it out, you know. So I bought this watch on time.

And then the man at this Fowler's Jewelry, he knew that we were the only people in there. So pretty soon he send the cops after us. And then they took us to the police station and then I said, "What's wrong?" The policeman says, "You guys were shoplifting." "What do you mean, shoplifting?" He says, "Yes, you guys stole a ring. So I'm going to take you to the detention home." And they took us to a big place, and they put us in until they would find the ring. And this Robert Hernández, he didn't want to say nothing about no ring. So they had us there for fifteen days.

And this Robert, they didn't put him where we were. They put him in a room by himself, just a little square room. And he was going crazy, you know. Pretty soon he started flushing the toilet so the water would run out. And so I used to call to him through the door, "Don't make too much noise or they're going to maybe hit you or something." And at that place they used to give us really nice things to eat. Really nice breakfast — canned peaches with cornflakes, and fried eggs with bacon.

My father came there to see me before my fifteen days were up, and right away, when I saw my father, I started crying. And then my father says, "What are you crying for?" Well, I cried because I saw my father and brother. I was small, and I started to cry. Right away my father says, "See, I told you a lot of times, don't hang around with those boys, and you still hang around with them." "Well," I told my father, "I won't do it no more, I know that." I just wanted him to get me out of there, you know. So pretty soon my father goes and talks to another man in San Bernardino that had better connections. My father couldn't speak English at all. But he went to another man that had a lot of connections and right away they took me out. Fifteen days I stayed there, and then they took me out of there. So then this man told me, "Don't hang around with those boys no more."

But I still used to hang around with them. This Robert Hernández, we used to call him Bob Alleluia because his father was a pastor. But Bob didn't go for that religion! Him and Quityeo both were Mexican, born in the States.

So pretty soon after that time in jail those guys come around and tell me, "Come on, let's go." And I told them, "My father gets mad. Don't come here." Sometimes my father would get really mad at one boy, "Camote" they used to call him; that is "Sweet Potato" in English. When my father got mad, he would chase him away, you know. And then Camote would come and call me at night, "Come on, let's go uptown." And I said, "No, you guys are going to get into trouble or something." He says, "No, we just going to look around." And we would go and look around.

One day Camote came to call me with Quityeo and this Bob Hernández, and they told me, "Let's go uptown." "OK." We went uptown and then we passed a restaurant. And there was a roast chicken turning on, you know, a rotisserie. He says, "You guys want some chicken?" I says, "Where are we going to get the money to eat chicken?" He says, "Come on, let's go." And we went in there and ordered chicken for each of us, and we ate a good chicken dinner. And then this other boy, this Quityeo, he pay. And then I thought, "Where does he get money?"

Then we passed by a store where they sold shoes. He says, "You want to buy yourself a pair of shoes?" I says, "Are you serious or are you just kidding?" "No, I'm serious." I says OK. So I went in there and got a new pair of shoes on. And he paid for the pair of shoes. And I started thinking, "Where did he get this money from?" I didn't know where he got the money, you know. But, well, I didn't pay no attention. Then he bought himself a shirt. He asked me, "You want a sweater?" And I says, "Yeah." So I bought a sweater. And then we went to the movies, and stuff like that all that day. Then we come home real late at night. And my father says, "Where were you?" I says, "We were uptown with Jesús."

Then the next day we went to school, and Mrs. Thorn was really mad. She says, "Somebody stole my money." Then it came to me where that money had come from. That was in the third grade.

The way she found out that Quityeo was the one that stole the money was because Quityeo left a valentine inside her purse. It was around Saint Valentine's Day, and Quityeo took the money out and left the valentine. On the valentine he put his name. The valentine was addressed to Mrs. Thorn from Jack Jesús Valdez. You know, if he would have took the valentine and the money, probably the teacher never would have found out who stole the money.

So then she called him, and she said, "Did you take my money?" And he says no. But he had. She told him, "Where did you get that new shirt?" And then she asked me where I got the new shoes. "I bought them. I didn't get into your purse." And then the teacher went and talked to Quityeo's father and told him he had to pay the money that his son had stolen. About fifty dollars! So his father paid the money because Jesús Valdez's father had a good job. He worked for the railroad. Mrs. Thorn didn't call the police; she just talked to the father, and the father decided to pay. At first Quityeo's father told my father he had to pay, too, for the shoes and everything. But then he said he didn't have to; he said he would do it all.

This Quityeo was really always getting into trouble. I remember one time when I went to his house his father had him tied to a chair with a chain on his leg. And I went over there and tried to break the chain, to turn him loose. And then his father came in and saw me, that I was breaking the chain, and he chained me to a chair, too. And we were chained there like dogs. Just for a little while, though. And then I told him, "Why don't you let us loose? We won't go no place." So he let us go.

This is the boy who used to steal his father's rabbits and sell them to go to the movies. His father had a lot of rabbits, and lots of times Quityeo would tell me, "You stand over there outside the fence, and I'll get a rabbit and throw it to you." You know, one of those white rabbits. And then we would go sell it to a woman and then we would go to the movies.

There used to be a movie there in San Bernardino called *Realto*. Most of the Mexican people would go to this movie, and we would go there to have a lot of fun. We used to take a lot of gum and sit in back where there would be girls, and we used to take the gum and put it in the girls' hair, and all that. Just to be mean to the girls. We used to pull the pigtails! And now they are all married, all these girls. Sometimes when I used to meet them, we would start talking about those days, even in front of their husbands. "Remember when you boys used to put gum in our hair and pull our pigtails?" "Oh yes." "You boys were really mean. But I remember a lot of times that we used to get gum and put it on you guys, too." Sometimes they used to put gum on us, and we had to get the scissors and cut our hair!

*   *   *

My Aunt María in San Bernardino sent me to a Catholic church school. I went to that school for about two years, I think it was for fourth and fifth grade. There in the school for the Catholic church they taught me how to pray. But I didn't like it there in Catholic school. Everyone was stricter than in public schools. I went every day and learned religion, arithmetic, and all that. Then I got out of there and went to a public school. But when you go to a public school the nuns, they go to the schools and wait for you to come out, and they take you to do your catechism. They teach you how to pray. So I still got some lessons on religion from the sisters.

But my aunt wanted me to get out of the public school, because she was very religious. She used to go to church in the morning and at night, and she used to say the rosary all the time in her hand. She was around forty, forty-three, something in her forties. And she was very strict. She wanted me to learn that religion, you know. And I told her, "Well, I like to learn, but not too much, only a little bit at a time." And she said, "No, you have to be religious like all of us." And I told her, "Well, if you want me to be religious like you, I will try, but I don't think I am going to be a good one."

I go to church, even now I go to church on Sunday. Not every Sunday, just once in a while, because I have not been very religious. Most people, they are very religious; they go to church every Sunday and maybe even every day. I only go once in a while. Most of the people in my town go to church every Sunday. But, see, their parents have taught them that, you know. They taught me that, too, but I never got very interested in becoming a Catholic.

*   *   *

You know, there in San Bernardino they used to call me "Cueco." My father used to get angry because they called me that. "Cueco" means a guy that limps. They called me that because I had this burn on my leg, and after I was burned I used to limp. I limped for maybe three years. Limped all the time. Just limped. It didn't hurt or anything.

It happened when I was crossing Sixth and Pickle Street one time in San Bernardino, and there was a man taking gasoline out of a tank of his car. He was smoking a cigarette, and a light fell into the tank as I was passing by. He kicked it, the gasoline, and the gasoline fell on my pants and started burning. And then I got scared and I started to run. And the man, named Joe Hernández, he ran after me and took his coat off and put the flames out with his coat. But then I had a lot of boils. I went home then, and my father asked me what was wrong. And I told him, "Nothing's wrong." So I went in and lay down, because of the pains. I put my leg into a great big bucket of water because the cold takes the pain away. Finally I couldn't stand it, and I told my father.

And my father went and got a gun, and he tried to kill this man because he burned me. But the man that burned me, he knew, so he took off for another town. My father took the gun and he went after this man and fired at the house, but the man wasn't there no more.

So finally my father came back, and he took me to a county hospital, you know. He took me to a hospital, and they poured alcohol or something on it and wet it. I stayed there in the hospital for maybe one month. I had my leg folded like this, and my leg got so stiff like that I couldn't stretch it no more. And then when I got out of the hospital, they gave me some crutches because I couldn't walk. They said that the nerve was stiff and they couldn't do nothing. And they told me the only way was for them to cut my leg. And I told them, "No, I'm not going to let them cut my leg." So they massaged it. They used to do that and stretch it out. And it hurt once you stretch it out. But you stretch it out and they massage it every day. But the first day the doctors they were saying they would have to cut it.

My father took me to a *curandera* from San Bernardino. A woman. Because in the States they have *curanderas* too, like here in Mexico. My leg is all right now, because she cured me! The only thing is this scar. It doesn't hurt me, you know. I can walk, run, everything.

Then another time . . . when men kill a pig, you know, they make *chicharrones,* cracklings you call them, and they eat them hot. Hot with tortillas, and you drink a lot of water, because the *chicharrones* are hot. And then all of a sudden I started feeling a pain in my belly. And the same *curandera,* she broke some eggs and put them on my belly. And then she says, "You know what's wrong with you? You're *empachado."* That means like when you eat pork meat, and they say your stomach gets real full, like you blow up in your belly. And she cured me of that, too. She's just like a witch, probably. Raw eggs she put on, two eggs. She put some kind of little herbs, you know. Towels she put on. And then she got me cured of that. It took maybe two weeks before I was cured. She worked on me every day, putting eggs and those herbs. And then pretty soon I start feeling all right.

*   *   *

When we were about thirteen or fourteen, this Quityeo and Bob Alleluia, we used to go around together all the time. We sold papers, and then we used to go around to a lot of neighborhoods. We used to go at night to see some girl, and these two boys were never afraid. We used to hang around together because, if a boy tried to jump us, then we all stick together. This boy, Bob Alleluia, he was good at fighting. He knew how to box.

One time we got into a fight with a bunch of guys. We ran and left this Bob behind, and he fought with those boys, and he beat the hell out of them. By himself! So finally, because he was so good at fighting, he decided to be a boxer. And he became a professional boxer. You get a book and see his name there in the records. You get out one of those encyclopedias where they have boxing, fighting; there's the name of Robert Hernández. He fought a lot of good guys, like maybe you heard of Nick Díaz from Los Angeles, and Dago, a Filipino.

Well, we used to hang around, you know, go around together. One time we were walking, and they took a wig out of a car. We were passing by on the sidewalk, and one of them saw a wig on a car seat, and he just put his hand in and took the wig out. And they were playing with it, you know. And then they gave it to me, and I threw it on top of a building, and we went home.

About three weeks passed, and then one day I was sleeping in my house when I saw a light in the window. I was just in my shorts. Then the police come in there and told me to get up. And I said, "What for? I haven't done nothing." They took me to the police station without shoes or anything, they just told me to put on my pants. I put my pants on, but then they took my shoes, I don't know why.

I saw this Quityeo there, and I says, "What happened?" He says, "That wig that we were playing with, it cost one thousand dollars." And they asked me, "Where did you throw that wig?" "We threw it on top of a building, I don't know, maybe it's still there." And they took us over there to show them where we threw that wig. They put a ladder, and they went up there and got that wig down. Then they let us go and told us, "OK, take off."

Those boys, they were my real buddies. We used to visit girls together, just to talk, you know, and go to each other's homes. Quityeo, his mother was very nice, and she used to cook for us, and I used to stay overnight at his house. We all three used to stay there. But this other boy, Alleluia, we didn't go to his house much, because his father was a Protestant preacher, and he was very strict.

We used to have a club and a clubhouse where we used to meet, and we used to keep all kinds of records, what we did, stuff like that. Finally we started growing up, and Alleluia, he went to some other town, and then I moved to Mendota, and it broke up. But every time I went back there I used to go visit them. Alleluia had four fingers cut off with one of those electric saws. He was cutting wood. He cut the whole fingers off. And my other buddy, Quityeo, he got married . . . not married, he just lived with a woman. One day this woman stuck a knife into his spine, and he is paralyzed. When he got drunk, she got even with him and stuck a knife in his back. And now he's paralyzed.

4. Adolescence

When I was about sixteen years old we moved from Mendota to
Woodlake. Woodlake is a town in Fresno County. No, I think it's in
Visalia County. It's a city known as an olive city, where they have
olives and oranges and grapefruit. My father decided to move there
because a lot of his friends were there. It was about eighty miles,
probably, from Mendota, or more. In Woodlake I went to about two
years of high school. I didn't finish high school.

And then I went to work there. I began to pick oranges and got
pretty good at picking oranges. I picked with my father, and then I
used to pick more than my father did! And we picked not only
oranges. The Japanese used to farm a lot of tomatoes, and you know
how the Japanese like to plant a lot of fruit, like tomatoes, onions,
garlic, stuff like that. The labor wasn't too high. It was only twenty-
five cents an hour, but that was a good wage in them days, twenty-
five cents.

I used to drive a truck hauling oranges, too. And then we would
be picking tomatoes, bell peppers, and then we used to work in those,
you know, eggplant. See, the Japanese they farm eggplant, celery,
cabbage, then they farmed those things . . . I forget the name . . .
cauliflowers! We worked for the Japanese on all those things, but
for the Americans it was mostly oranges. That's the kind of work I
did in them days after I quit school.

You know, in Woodlake the houses were made of concrete, and
they were all close to each other, like an apartment. But those houses
belonged to the ranch that we worked on, and they didn't charge you
no rent or nothing. They just let you live there because you were
working for the ranch. They give you a house to live in. The house

was one room, and then a kitchen, a shower, and a sink where you can wash your face or do dishes if you want to. In that kitchen we used to have a wood stove, and then in the room where we used to sleep, we had three beds there. But it was very cold, you know, because it was all cement. Very damp. That's the coldest that I ever lived.

One time when I was seventeen or eighteen I ran away from home with another boy. We hitchhiked from Woodlake to Los Angeles. When we were hitchhiking we got so tired we decided to get a hike on a railroad train. So we got on the train and we got to Los Angeles, and then we were lost in the big city. Just me and him, and we didn't know where to go and we were all dirty; our pants were all dirty. The town we were headed for was San Pedro — he had a married sister who was living there. So we got into the middle of L.A., and we walked and walked a whole lot, just walking, walking, to get to San Pedro. We asked somebody where San Pedro was, and he said we had to have money to get a bus. So finally we crossed a lot of fields and we got to a town named Wilmington. We walked all night and then we asked someone, "Where is San Pedro?" "Oh, it is only about eight miles more." And we walked clear over there.

About five in the morning we got there to San Pedro. We knocked on the door of this boy's sister and she bawled us out because we were all dirty. She says, "What are you doing here?" She wrote to her father, and he came for us and took us back in his car. He took us back to Woodlake, but before we got there he gave us a good going over with a belt! That was the first time that I took off with somebody like that, and the last time. When you take off like that by yourself, you suffer a lot. We didn't have any money at all. We just took off like that, crazy. We didn't know what we were doing.

*　*　*

It was after we moved to Woodlake that I got my first car. I must have been around fifteen or sixteen years old. My father bought it for me. It was an old Model-T Ford. I used to drive it, but I didn't have no driver's license. I only used to drive it around small towns like Woodlake, Exeter, Dinuba, and Selma. I used to drive in those small towns, but I never used to go to the big cities, like Fresno. I was afraid that they would pick me up without a driver's license. But I burned one piston on it, and they charged too much to fix it, so I decided not even to take it out of the garage. That Model-T Ford cost us only about forty dollars, and to fix it they wanted sixty dollars, so we let it go. Then my father says, "Well, let's buy another one." And we bought another one, a Chevie.

A '36 Chevie. And that '36 Chevie didn't last me very long. Because one day we went to Visalia to a movie, and then my father and another man they went to the cantina and started to drink in there. And me and my brother went to a movie. And when we came out of the movie, then we went to look for my father. And my father and this man were still in the cantina. They were fooling with the woman that sells the beer, the *cantinera*. And she was giving my father and this man the shakes and all that, and she says, "Let's dance." We were just there, looking in. And then me and my brother went and told my father, "Let's go," because it was about twelve o'clock already, midnight. And my brother told my father that we were sleepy. So my father said, "Well, go sleep in the car for a little while."

So we went and slept in the car for a little while and then I couldn't sleep so we got out again and went and told our father, "Come on, let's go." So finally he and this other man came out and we left. We were coming on down the road, and all of a sudden, about two miles before we got to our house, I fell asleep on the steering wheel. All I remember is that we were like going over bumps, and then I opened my eyes and I saw that I was going off the road into a big ditch. And there was a telephone pole right in front. And then I was going to turn the wheel to get back on the road, when my father got a hold of the steering wheel and twist it, you know. And all of a sudden the car started rolling, turning, so many times. It rolled over about three times, and then it rested on one side.

Then we all got out of the car and my father was so mad, cussing so much and saying "Look what you did," and all that. And then this other man had a cut right here in the face. So we got out of the car, and it was all wrecked up. The car was no good for nothing. So then I told my father, "Well, we have to go to the insurance, maybe get it fixed." And then they said they couldn't fix it, but they would give us another one. And then we got another car, I think it was a '36 too, but a sedan, not a coupe.

With that car with the two seats I used to go with a friend of mine out to a ranch to pick up two girls. So one day this girl told me, "Let me drive." And I was afraid to let her drive because she didn't know how to drive. But she was a girl I liked, so finally I let her drive. I had my arm around her, and I was scared. Pretty soon she was on top of a tree. I got so mad, I told her, "Now see what you've done!" She hit a tree and broke one light, and then one fender was bent. And I didn't want to take it like that to my father.

So we went to a place where they estimated how much they would charge to straighten the fender and fix that light. He told us, "Everything for sixty dollars." And you know, we didn't have no money, but we told him, "Well, fix it, we'll try to get the money some way." So me and this boy, we went to work. We raised the money by Saturday and then we went and paid. The car was all fixed, and my father didn't know about it, that I wrecked the car.

That car, I traded it in for a '41 Plymouth, and that '41 Plymouth I bought in Fresno. I had it for quite a while. And we used to go around with it, to Mendota, to Stockton, to Sacramento. That Plymouth, it turned out to be real good.

Then one day we were on our way down a mountain in California. As we were driving down the slope, all of a sudden I seen a wheel going in front of me. A wheel by itself! And I told my brother, "Look at that wheel!" And then I step on the brakes to pick that wheel up, and all of a sudden the car falls down. And then we look at the wheel, and where they have the bolts, it was ripped off. The whole thing ripped off. So I told my brother, "Well, you have to go to Fresno and get another wheel." So my brother went to Fresno and got another wheel, and that car, we traded it in for another one. We trade it in for a Ford, maybe one year older, maybe a '40. And that Ford, we kept it for quite a while. When it broke down I used to fix it.

Then I bought an old one, an old 1928 Nash, and the Nash burned a lot of gas. I would put gas and fill the tank and then go around and pretty soon it was almost empty. When I had this Nash I was living in Hollister. An uncle of mine named Raymond lived there, and we used to go pick girls up in this old Nash. I remember this one girl they used to call Birdie, an American girl, we used to go pick her up and take her out. And then this car, I finally sold it to, I think a cousin of mine, and then I moved to Watsonville.

There in Watsonville I got this Mercury. That was a 1950 Mercury. And that 1950 Mercury was very good, but then my brother said, "How come we don't buy a new car?" So that's what we did. And I traded this Mercury in for a 1956 Plymouth, and this Plymouth turned out very good, too.

One time I went to Ventura and got me a driver's license. That's the first time I ever got a driver's license. I must have been around eighteen. I drove for maybe five years without a driver's license. It was against the law, but you know, a lot of people, they do it even if it's against the law. But when I didn't have a driver's license I never got a ticket, and then when I got the license, the second day that I got it, I got me a ticket. When I had no driver's license I used to drive maybe more carefully.

You know, it was hard to get a driver's license. Because one time I went to try and get a license in Fresno. And they have a man there in Fresno that you pay five dollars and he will help you get your driver's license. And I couldn't get it even though he was helping me, because when this policeman got in the car to drive around, I got all nervous. And then there was a fire hydrant and he told me, "Stop here," and I stopped because he was a policeman and he told me to stop there. Then he asked me, "How come you stop there?" "Well," I said, "you told me to stop." So he told me they couldn't give me no driver's license because I didn't know the safety rules. I didn't go back no more, then. Then I tried it by myself without nobody helping me.

I went to that town named Ventura. They gave me a paper with a lot of questions to fill out. And then I filled out the paper and he told me that I passed the test. And then he told me, "Come tomorrow about nine o'clock so you can have your other test." So the next day the police got inside the car. We turned around the block, and then he told me, "Park here." And I parked and then he told me, "OK, let's go." And then he told me to do the signals. You know, you put your hand out and all that. And then we went back and he said "OK," and he gave me a temporary license. I passed! From then on I had a driver's license. I renewed it twice. Every time you renew you have to drive. Not take a test, just drive around. I don't have it any more. It expired, so I don't have it.

*   *   *

When I was younger, I used to have a lot of fights. Fist fights, not with knives, only with fists. I remember one time that I fought with one guy in San Bernardino. I fought with him for half an hour. I must have been around seventeen. I was fighting with this guy, and I was beating this guy all up, and the father of the boy came up and told his son, "If you stop fighting, I'm going to beat you up." So the boy didn't want to stop. So he kept on fighting and fighting, and finally we were all tired, so this boy says, "Let's rest." I says "OK, let's rest." We rest, then we got into fighting again. So we were all black eyes, and all blood all over us, and then his father finally said, "Well, I think that's enough for you boys." And I told his father, "I think so too." And we stopped fighting and the next day I saw this boy, and he told me, "We were so lucky, my father said for us to stop it. Look at my eyes," he says. And I says, "Yeah, look at mine, my eyes, too." I had two black eyes, and I rip his lids. And we were all clean fighting, no kicking or nothing. Boxing, like that. That's one fight that I will never forget!

Another time I was fighting a guy, you know, and I was beating him up, and then one of his brothers jumped in. And then my brother jumped in. We were fighting two brothers against two brothers. I must have been around twenty-three, I think. And then my brother, he beat his guy up real quick, the brother of this guy that I was fighting. He's a good fighter, you know, my brother. So he fought this guy and he beat him quick, and me and this guy we stood there about one hour fighting, and we would get tired and then we would rest, and then we would go again. So finally he said, "I think that's enough." I says, "OK," and then we shake hands and he says we're still buddies.

And then another time I fought with a Negro. I must have been around nineteen. This was at the border, the border of California and Mexico. Well, I got into a fight with him because one day I was walking down the street with a girl, her name was María Gómez. We were walking down the street, and this Negro told this girl how beautiful she was and all that, kind of wisecracks. I didn't say nothing. We just took off.

And then later I told this guy we called Burro, I said, "Burro, let's go out and look for this Negro." He says, "What for?" "Oh," I told him, "when we pass, me and this girl, he start saying a lot of things. Let's go tell him not to do that no more." I was just going to tell him not to say all those things when I go by. I was mad because this girl said, "How come you don't say anything?"

So me and Burro went there and I told this guy, the Negro, they call him Tuna, I ask him, "Hey, Tuna, how come you said that in front of this girl?" And I told him, "Don't do it again." And he told me, "You know what? Every time you pass I'm going to tell her anything I like, and nobody's going to stop me." So I told him, "You know what? You do that again, I'm going to beat you up." He says, "You can't do nothing." He was about my age, but he looked more, you know, husky, you know how the Negroes are. They look very husky. So I says OK, and we took off.

But then the next time I was walking with a girl, he started saying things again. So then I told the girl, "You walk in front, I want to tell this guy something." So I hit the Negro, you know, I hit him in the face. And he came back to hit me, and I kicked him in the shins. Because I heard that the Negroes, that's their weakest part. A lot of people told me that. Mexican boys, they told me that if you ever got in a fight with a Negro, kick him in the shins. And I kick him there and right away he started getting ahold of his shins. So I hit him in the face and all over the body. Then I left him there, and I took off. He wasn't really hurt, just black eyes, like that. He didn't get a chance to hit me nothing at all.

And then the next day he saw me, he talked to me, and he said that he was sorry for all the trouble that he was trying to do to me. So I told him, "That's nothing." I used to work for his father on the lettuce, cleaning lettuce, carrots, and onions. His father was a fore-man. His father used to have a place where they load watermelons. They would load watermelons into boxcars and then ship them to L.A., to San Francisco, different parts.

*   *   *

One time in Woodlake I went on a double date with a boy and his girl friend. But I didn't know the girl that was going along with me that night. He asked me, "You want to go on a blind date?" I told him, "I don't know." I told him I didn't know what to say to this girl, and he told me maybe in the daytime I should practice what I was going to say. And you know, when I got there, I forgot everything I was going to say to the girl. I forgot everything. I didn't know what to say. I didn't even open my mouth to tell her hello or something.

And I let this boy drive my car, and him and his girl got in the front seat, and we got in the back seat. And we were there and then I put my arm around this girl. She didn't say anything, and then I asked her what was her name. And then she told me her name, and pretty soon we were very friendly.

Then we went to a dance at the high school in Woodlake. So I asked her, "Do you want to go inside to the dance?" And she said, "No, I would rather stay outside here and talk to you." And I said, "Well, OK," so we stayed there. And I told her to get out of the car, but she didn't want to get out of the car; she wanted to stay inside. So I got back in and we stayed there and the other guys went into the school, to the dance. Finally, they came out and we took the girls home, and I kind of liked this girl.

And every time I used to go to her house she was sitting down. She was very beautiful, she was half Mexican and half American, and she was good-looking. But when I would go there at night she was always sitting down. And that used to puzzle me, how come she was sitting down all the time.

She had a cousin named Gabe and finally one day I asked him, "How come she never wants to stand outside or come outside when I leave? She stays inside the house; she don't come and leave me at the car or something like that." So finally this guy told me what was wrong with her. "You know why she don't like for you to see her? It is because one foot is bigger than the other, and she limps, that's why."

The next time I went to see her — because I didn't care if she limped, she was good-looking — I said, "Why don't you walk with me to the car?" "No," she says, "I'm too tired." And I told her, "I don't care if you're too tired. I know why you don't want to go out to the car with me, because you limp a little bit. But that's all right, you can come." She says she didn't want to tell me, she didn't want to lose me or something like that. But she was good-looking, you know. And I kept going there for quite a while. Finally we had to move from there, me and my father, we had to move from Woodlake to another town. And then I never came back to see her. And she said she liked me so much and all that. That's the only blind date that I ever went on. It worked out all right. But at first I thought it was kind of hard to go on a blind date.

One girl that I used to love so much was a girl in Clovis. Even though I didn't marry her, she was just my girl. Even now I still think about her a lot. Because I used to love her so much. She was my sweetheart. I was so crazy about her that I used to get drunk every day because I was going to lose her. She was a student in Fresno State.

When I knew her she was nineteen. She had been in college for maybe one year. She was nice. She wanted to get married with me, but she said she was going to finish college first. She used to go with me in my car and everything. She's not the one that smashed up my car, no. This girl was more . . . just for thinking about her for getting married, not for fooling around. These other girls . . . you used to pick them up just for fooling around. But this one I didn't fool around. Just talked to her, and then I would just kiss her, like that, you know. Not do anything bad to her, nothing like that. I was thinking more that I would marry her in the right way.

I first met her because I knew two girls there in that town. I must have been around twenty-two. I went around with her for two years. I begin to love her so much that I . . . even though I am now married and have met other girls, I still think of this girl. I think if I had married her, I would have been better off. But it was just one of those things. I broke up with her because she told me to wait four years for her to get out of college. She was going to Fresno State College. She was going to be a school teacher. And then I told her, "Oh, by the time you get out of college I could be married twenty times." And she got mad. She got mad, and finally I told her, "Well, that's all right, you can go to college." And then I took off.

Then I was in Fresno one day, and I saw her coming down the street. And I didn't want to see her, so instead of meeting her on the street, I crossed the street so I wouldn't see her. But I know I made a mistake, because I loved her so much. I never went back to see her because I had too much pride. That's why I never went. Even guys that knew me said I was crazy. Because they said that girl was very nice. And that she was. They said I was crazy to leave her. I didn't want to wait!

She was a Mexican girl; her parents were born in Michoacán, and she was born in the States. Her father was very friendly, and the mother too. To that girl's family I used to go by myself every night. Well, sometimes they didn't invite me, but I would go. I would go there and knock on the door and then they would see who it was and they would tell me, "Come in." And I would sit down and eat with them. They treat me really good, real nice. They only had that one daughter. They treat me like I was one of the family. They served me whatever food I liked. That felt good, you know, because I used to say to myself, "Well, these people like me." Like if I was their son.

And she used to tell me, "My folks like you." She used to tell me that. Well, I liked them too; that's why I used to buy food or something and take it to them. And you know how during the war they used to give you books of stamps? Well, I used to get the book of stamps, and I used to give the meat stamps to them because I didn't need them. That was 1944, 1945, something like that. I used to give her the meat stamps, and I used to keep the shoe stamps.

One time that I remember I went and bought a gallon of wine, because I knew her father liked wine. And I went to her house and invited her father to drink with me. And she was mad with me because I was drinking with her father. Finally her father got drunk and fell asleep, and I fell asleep in the car.

I loved her so much that I used to visit her every day. I used to live on a ranch, and it was about five miles to her house from the ranch. And I used to get a ride to her house in the truck of the man that I used to work with, and then I used to walk back at night. Five miles every night! Every night I used to go see her. And then sometimes I used to get home at one o'clock in the morning to where I lived. Oh, I used to love her so much that I used to go see her every day without missing one day. Oh, that was the girl of my life. I think I love her more than my wife. Because my wife, this wife I have now, I love her too, but I mean, this girl was kind of the best one I have ever gone with.

5. First Deportation

I left home about a year before my father was deported. I was about eighteen or nineteen. My father moved back to Mendota and then to San Bernardino again, and from there he got deported to Mexico. So my brother went one way, and I went another way. I went to this town named Madera. See, they farm a lot of grapes there, a lot of different kinds of grapes. I was picking grapes there, making a good wage. I didn't even know that my father was deported until later. I get along with my father very good, even now, you know.

In 1943 my father was deported from the United States because they passed a law that you have to register as an alien in the States. When they told my father that he had to register as an alien, he moved to San Bernardino, because in San Bernardino my father knew an Immigration officer. The Immigration people there told my father that he had to register at a certain time, and then my father did not register at this certain time, so they deported him to Mexico. They just brought him to the border in Mexicali, and then my father took a train to his town. But I didn't know he was deported, because I was in jail.

*　　*　　*

I got put in jail in about 1942. I got put in jail in San Jose when I was hanging around with an Italian guy. Every day we used to go and try out a different car at one of those places where they sell used cars. He used to say he was going to try it out like he was going to buy it, you know.

So one time we tried a car, and then he said, "Oh, let's not take it back." And I told him, "OK, I just follow you." So we went from

California to another state with that car, to South Dakota. We went to South Dakota with that car, and we kept it for six months. Then he said, "Well, let's go back to California, they have forgotten about this car, we will just take it back and paint it another color."

As soon as we crossed the border into California, right away they picked us up. And they brought us to the county jail in San Jose. There they put the charges: grand theft. They sent this other guy to San Quentin for one to fifty years, I think it was. They gave me nine months in jail. I didn't stay there the whole nine months, only about seven months. They give you five days a month for good behavior, so they let me out early on good behavior.

I didn't stay in the county jail the whole time. The last part I stayed out in the country on a farm. They called it a jail farm, and I used to farm and cut wood, and maybe plant tomatoes, and all of those things. They grow the food for the men in the jail. But it was nice out on the farm, because you have more freedom. You get out in the open, that's why it is nice.

But first I was in the county jail in San Jose about three months. It was just a big room and a lot of beds — there were about two hundred guys or more in that one room. It had a door, and it's locked all the time. They had showers, bath, everything. Then in a corner they had a big stove. In case anybody came to see you and bring groceries and things like that, you cook them on that stove. Besides that, we cooked our regular meals on that stove. That jail used to have real good food there.

In the daytime we used to sleep most of the time. Then later on we used to get up, and a lot of people stayed up way in the night, playing cards or playing dice. But I was so young that I didn't know how to play those games. But one time a relative of mine came to see me, and he left me some money. So these guys knew that I had some money, and they invited me to play dice. They wanted to win the money that I had, they wanted to beat me out of the money. So I told them OK. And this one man, a little short man named Ceciero — he had a broken nose — he threw me the dice.

Then these guys said, "How much do you want to bet?" I think I had around fifteen dollars. And I threw the fifteen dollars down. I just wanted them to leave me alone. And one man, he put down fifteen dollars. He had more, but he wanted to get my fifteen dollars. So right away I throw, and I put a seven and I win. I won thirty dollars. And this man says, "OK, the thirty." I says, "OK, the thirty," and I threw and put another seven. And I did that for about seven times. And then this man that had the broken nose got the dice and told me, "That's enough. Don't play no more." And I says, "OK." And I don't play no more. That day I won close to two hundred dollars. And then he told me to give him twenty-five dollars, this man. Because the dice that he had given me were not straight dice; they were loaded dice. But I didn't know. He was a gambler, I guess. He did that because they try to beat me from the money. Pretty soon I began to like to play dice too, and I used to pass the time playing dice or poker with them, or "twenty-one."

They used to have fights in there once in a while. They had Mexicans and Americans in there, and they had colored, too. A lot of guys there were colored, like the cook of the jail. He was in jail, too, but he was a cook, and he was very mean. See, they used to give you three slices of bread, but this colored guy only give two slices to this one Mexican boy, and this Mexican didn't like it. So he got in a fight with this cook. This cook, he was supposed to have been a prize-fighter. And this Mexican, he was not a fighter, but he was pretty stocky, pretty husky. We used to call him *Huskiamo,* and he became a fighter later on.

And this Mexican hit this colored man and knocked him down about three times. And this colored boy, he cut the Mexican's eye. He cut him up. The jailers, the policemen, they wouldn't stop the fight. They were just looking. So finally one of them decided they had fought enough. He stopped them. Then the jailers went inside. They respected this Mexican guy; he was the only one that would stand up against this colored cook.

*   *   *

Just before I got out of jail the Immigration came and told me my father was deported because he didn't register. I didn't register either, so I got deported in May of 1943. From San Jose they took me to San Francisco, and then to an Immigration camp. And there I stayed for I think it was three months. You know, there's a lot of red tape before they can process you. They ask a lot of questions and all that.

At the Immigration camp I was in the big barracks there. There was a lot of guys. There must have been over a thousand of them in there. And all kinds of nationalities, like the Mexicans, Russians, Germans, different nationalities. They call it "Immigration facilities." They had a big kitchen in there where you go in a file to eat. Like when you are in the army, and you get your tray, and they serve you and everything.

After breakfast you come out, and then if you want to work, well, you can work and they give you maybe five dollars or ten dollars a week. So I used to work there, in the general construction they called it. They used to have a machine that makes cement, a cement mixer. It was really nice in that camp, you know. They had a store inside where you could buy things. They had a big playground where you could play baseball or touch football.

Every morning they would put up a list of guys that would be deported that day. And every morning about eleven o'clock we used to go look at the list to see which boys would be deported. The train would leave every day about one o'clock. If your name was not on there, you felt sad because you weren't going to be deported, because you wanted to get out. You were real heartbroken because you were going to stay there some more days. But soon I got used to it. I didn't even go look at the list, I waited until they call your name on the microphone, I heard the names on the microphone, so I wouldn't go look at the list no more.

So I passed the time playing cards or out playing baseball. When they used to play baseball, they used to call me, "Come on, let's go play." "Oh no, I want to rest a while." "Oh, come on, let's go play baseball." Because when they know you can play, right away they want you on their team. "Come on so you can be on my team." "OK." So we went and played baseball; every day we used to play. And pretty soon you seem like you're at home.

And the Immigration, sometimes they take you to a city. We used to go to the movies with this Immigration officer. About nine of us. He used to ask us, "Do you have any money?" And we say yes. "Well, OK, I'm going to take you to the movies," he says. And we used to go because he was going to bring the groceries back. And he used to say, "Don't run off or else I get in trouble." So we'd go to the movies with him, but we never run off. If we want to go someplace, he used to take us around. He was nice to us, you know.

So finally my name was on the list. I think it was in May that I was deported. And then they took us to San Francisco on the train, and there in San Francisco they got us on the train to El Paso, Texas.

One day and a half it took us to get to El Paso, thirty-six hours I think it was. I don't remember exactly, but it took a long time, through the mountains and everything. And then they give us a little bag of sandwiches for the meals. In certain towns that they pass, I guess they pick the sandwiches up. Towns like Needles, Arizona, and all those places we were passing. It was very hot, you know. And finally we got to El Paso.

And there in El Paso they didn't put us in jail. They just took us out of the train to the border. The Immigration turned us over to the Mexican parties. There were maybe 100, 120 of us, something like that.

I didn't have no money, you know. I only had about fifty cents in American money. That's all I had. And then they turn us over to the Mexicans and everybody went his way. Me and another boy, I forget his name, we went together and I told him I only had fifty cents. He says, "Well, I have fifty cents, and I'm going to eat with this fifty cents." And we went to a little restaurant they call Monterrey Restaurant, and we ate there.

After that I went and sold a ring I had; I got about ten pesos for the ring. Then I went to a place where you can send telegraphs, and I was going to put a telegraph there to my home town in Mexico, to my father or my grandfather, so they could send me some money so I could get there.

You know, when I was there I saw two bundles of money laying on the floor, in the telegraph office. There was another man there putting a telegraph, maybe he dropped them or something. And I kneeled down and I got the two bundles and I put them in my pockets. And I walked out of the telegraph office. I didn't even put the telegram.

Then I went to this room where I had hocked my jacket so they would let me stay in the room. Before I found the money I told him, "I have no money. I only have this leather jacket." He let me stay there until I get some money, some work, or something. And then I came back and I told the man, "Can I have my jacket? I'll pay you for the room." One thing I didn't know was how much the money was good for in Mexico, how much it was worth. Well, I left two ten peso bills, "Here, for that room." And I said to myself, well, if he takes it it means it's good. So he took them, and he gave me two pesos in change. And I said to myself, "They're good!"

And then I went out and I went to a place where they sell suits.

And I said, "How much is that suit?" And he told me 180 pesos for a suit, in them days. And that money, it was worth more. It was 4.8 pesos to the American dollar then, but now it is 12.5. So I tried it on, then a shirt, and then a tie. I got all dressed up, because I didn't want to go home looking like a tramp.

Then I bought me a suitcase, and I put my things in there. I went to the depot, and I bought a ticket to Irapuato. I think it cost me thirty-four pesos. I never saw anything like it, you know. When we get on the train, a lot of people come around trying to sell you something. And I was having a lot of fun, buying something through the window — cokes, sodas, anything. And then I would fool around with the girls. I'd tell them, "You want to come with me to Irapuato?" And sometimes I'd be talking to them and the train would leave, and I wouldn't pay them. And they would run after the train and tell you to pay.

So finally I got to Irapuato. At Irapuato I got off, and I was scared, quite scared, because I didn't know where to go. So there in the depot I asked one man how to get to my home town, Pueblo Nuevo. "Well," he told me, "it's too far from here for you to walk, you got to get a bus. You go straight over there and you'll find some buses that go there." And then I took the bus to my home town.

* * *

When I got off there, the people, as soon as they saw me, they start closing the doors on me. Because they thought I was a doctor. See, there was a man that came to vaccinate the people there, because not long ago here in Mexico they had a big disease of cattle. People from the United States came here, and they killed a lot of cattle. So they thought I was a doctor and I was going to vaccinate people.

I asked a bus driver where my grandfather lived, and he said, "Over there by those little trees." Then when they saw me, my aunt, she was my father's sister, she closed the door on me. And I knocked and says, "Open the door. It's me." She says, "Who? Who is me?" And I says, "Ramón." And then she finally called my father. My father looks through a little hole in the door and says, "Open the door, this is Ramón!" So they open the door, and I went in. After they let me in they told me that they had closed the door because they thought that I was a doctor.

And my father's sister she was young, she was around . . . well, not too old, she was around twenty-two years old. And she begin to like me very good. I promised her that I would send her a fur coat from the States when I got back. After I came back to the States I used to have correspondence with her very often.

Then one time after I was back in the States I wrote to her and told her in the letter that I was in the hospital. I was in the hospital because I broke my teeth in an auto accident. And then she got all scared, and she was kind of sick or something. A lot of people claim that she was sick of *calentura,* a fever, because of me.

They gave her one of those injections for making the fever come down, but this injection went into poison, and she died of that. A lot of people claim that she got sick because she worried that I was in the hospital, and that's why she died. But I think it wasn't because of that; she died of the injection. The doctor gave the injection, but it wasn't good. She wanted to go to church, and she had an injection so that she would be cured right away.

See, here in Mexico, people have funny beliefs. Like one of these women, if you're sick or something, right away they feel somebody is doing something to you, that one of those witches, a *hechicera* is what they call them, is doing something to you. And then you have to go to another woman, a *curandera,* to get your cure, and that woman is just taking your money. She's not getting you cured. She charge you eighty pesos now, eighty pesos tomorrow, like that. She's just taking your money!

6. More Trouble With the Law

Anyway, after I was in Mexico about six months I came back to the border. At the border there were a lot of other guys who had been deported too. They said, "Let's go back, let's jump the fence." I says, "They will try to catch us." "No," they said, "they won't catch us." "OK," I said, and we jumped the border, me and two other boys. We jumped the border in Tijuana, and we came to San Diego.

Then in San Diego — those boys didn't know how to speak English — so I said, "You boys stay over here in case the Immigration comes," and I bought three tickets on a Greyhound bus to Los Angeles. Then I bought a newspaper, an American newspaper. We got on the bus, and they sat at the far end, and I sat at a different seat. I was reading the American newspaper when the Immigration got in the bus and asked for your identification, about halfway between San Diego and Los Angeles. But because I was reading the American newspaper, they didn't ask me for no identification. Then they went over to the other two guys and took them off the bus.

Then in L.A., when I got off there, I called my brother David on the phone. He was in Watsonville, so I called him up and told him to come pick me up in L.A. He came with his car, him and a cousin of mine; and they picked me up and took me to Watsonville.

See, my brother, he was born in the States. So in 1943, when

me and my father were deported, he stayed in the States with relatives
in San Bernardino. Then he moved to San Jose with an uncle of
mine, José Hernández, and later on he went to Watsonville.

*   *   *

In 1944 I got in trouble with the law in Fresno. I knew some
Mexican boys there; they had jumped the border too. They never
worked, see, these boys just steal and stuff like that. And I used to
ask them, "How come you boys don't work?" They would say, "We
just work at night, you want to come with us?" "Well, I just like
to go see how you guys make your money."

So we go down the street. Pretty soon they told me, "Wait for
us on the corner." I says OK. So I stayed there and they went to the
parking lot of a big hotel. There was a lot of cars there, you know.
Pretty soon they come with three suitcases full of clothes. And I go
over and say, "So this is how you guys make your money." And then
they said, "You know what you can do? The place where you stay,
you can ask them if they would like to buy all these clothes from us."

So we're talking there, and all of a sudden two policemen cross
the street. And when they crossed, I ran. I ran like a rabbit. And
those guys, they threw their suitcases at the policemen and ran too.
And I was running, and there was a big fence about ten feet or higher,
I don't know. I don't know how I jumped it, but I jumped the fence.

I was so scared, and I jumped. When I fell over, there was a
lot of water, mud, and everything. And I fell in there. I heard the cops
say, "I saw him come to here, but I don't think he jumped here
because this fence is too high. It's impossible for a man to jump it."
And he says, "Even if one of us tried to get up there, we couldn't get
up there." So he says, "No, he didn't go through here." So they took
off, and I stayed there for maybe one hour. And I was all full of mud
and everything.

That was the second time I really got in trouble with the law,
I was so scared. They fire with a gun, you know. Well, I don't think
they shot at us. They shot about four shots, but they probably shot
just in the air because they didn't want to hit us.

After all that I got out and I went to my room. I went to take
a shower, because all my clothes were full of mud and everything.
And I told those guys, "I'll never go with you again like that to see
what you are doing. I had better stay here." And those guys say, "You
let us stay in your room." I says, "OK, I let you stay in my room."

And I had a lot of clothes hanging on the wall. And I says, "Well, I have to go to work. I'm going to go pick grapes, and you guys, you can stay here. You leave the key at the desk." And you know, when I came back from work I looked in my room and it was empty — no clothes or nothing. They cleaned me out! They only left me one pair of shoes. They were under the bed. They probably didn't look under the bed, or they would have took that too. A pair of shoes and one pair of pants there were. A pair of pants and some that were in the cleaners. That's all they left me. But everything else they cleaned me out. And I was so mad that I wanted to know where they were. I wanted to go beat them up or do something to them.

And finally one boy he came, about three days later, and told me, "You know what? I saw your friends," And I says, "Where?" "In Bakersfield. They're selling your clothes." So I told the guy that had the car, "Let's go to Bakersfield. I'll give you money for the gas and everything." It was not far; it was about 105 miles from Fresno to Bakersfield.

As soon as these guys saw me coming in, they tried to run. But they couldn't run because we had closed the doors, and we were in the way of them coming out. So I told them, "Look, I'm not going to beat you up. We're not going to do nothing. Just give me my clothes back." And they told me, "We sold them." I says, "Where?" And we went over there to this restaurant, and I told the lady, "You know the clothes this boy sold you? They are mine! Would you give them back to me?" Then the lady said she gave them, I think it was five dollars. Then I told the lady, "OK, I'll give you the five dollars. Give me the clothes." And she gave me the clothes. So then this guy told me, "Why don't you slap them one? Just slap them once." I says, "These guys ain't nothing." So we let them go and took all my clothes back. They had cleaned me out of every little thing in clothes. And you know, about two months later I read in the papers these boys had stolen some things, and they were sentenced to San Quentin for five years.

*　*　*

The next time I got in trouble was in the winter of 1949, about December I think. There was no work at all in Fresno. No work at all. All the factories had closed for Christmas. They stay closed during that time, and they open again around January. Nothing to pick, you know. And this one boy says, "How are we going to pay our rent? We have to find work or do something." Me and this boy, Tony Corales, we were living together. He was from Mexico, too.

And he says, "Well, you know what? We can do what those boys were doing. We go to a car and we open it." I says, "How are we going to open a car when it's locked?" He says, "Well, it's easy to open them, because I went with those guys once." He says, "We get a screwdriver and we open the little window." "Yeah," I told him, "you know what? If they catch us, you know what they are going to do? Send us to San Quentin." "No," he says, "they won't send us to San Quentin. They will just deport us." So I says, "OK, they deport us. It's better to be deported than to live like this anyway."

So we went. But we didn't know how to do it, so we couldn't get nothing out of the cars. But finally we got one car opened. And he got just a topcoat. It was the only thing inside. And then we sold the topcoat, and we paid our rent. I says, "Now we don't have to go anymore. If we go, we get caught and we get deported."

But you know, we wanted to get deported. We used to go walk by the Immigration to see if they would ask us for papers or anything. But they wouldn't ask us for nothing. And we wanted to get deported.

Finally we got caught by the police for taking that topcoat. And they told us, "You know what? That's a felony. That is grand theft." I says, "Who invented that? We didn't steal a car or something." "Yeah, but don't you know that breaking into something, that's against the law?" If the car had been open instead of locked, that would have been a misdemeanor. They told us, "Well, you're going to go before the judge." And then the judge sentenced me to one to fifteen years. But I didn't do much of that time. I only done one year and six months. And I got out. Because you go before a board there, and they fix your time for good behavior and all that.

Well, when you go into prison they give you a lot of tests to see how bright you are. They do that to a lot of those nuts, you know, that are crazy. And they have little blocks, and letters that you have to fix. You do that for three months. You have a lot of arithmetic too, so they can figure out what kind of grade they can put you in, because they have schools there, inside. So we went there for about three months. Finally they decided how bright you are and all that and they figure you're OK in your head; that you're not kind of crazy, you know!

They have, you know, a psychiatrist. They look at you and they study you, I guess. They talk to you. For twenty-five minutes like that to each guy, every day. Every day you go to him, and he talks to you and sees your reactions. Finally they decide what barrack you go in. He says, "Now this guy, he passes," and they take you to a certain barrack. And if he thinks you're a little off, he sends you to D-wing. D-wing is a barrack where they keep you locked all the time. They take the food there to you because they figure you're a little crazy.

And then when I was there, in the barrack where I was, one guy named John López, he killed two guys with a knife. He killed them because he just, he was crazy, you know. But when you used to talk to him you didn't think he was crazy. A lot of people used to tell me, "Don't get too near to him because he's crazy." But I didn't think so. So I used to talk to him nights. And then he killed those guys.

It was early in the morning, about eight o'clock, and I was sleeping about three beds from him when he got up and killed these two guys. I didn't know they were dead, but he killed a Mexican and this Negro, and he cut up another Negro. He must have got mad with them the day before, and he didn't forget it. When I saw him come I got the mattress, and I put it in front of me. I thought, if he comes at me with the knife like that, I put the mattress. But he tell me, "You know what? I don't kill you because you're my friend."

Pretty soon a lot of the cops come in and they told him to drop the knife. He dropped the knife, a big knife. They took him and put him in a little cell, and they used to take the food to him and put it through. Then one day he went to court. Jail used to have court every Tuesday. They tried him for murder, and the last time I heard of him he was given life, because they couldn't put him in the gas chamber. They couldn't put him in a gas chamber because the doctors said he was crazy. So maybe he's still there.

Well, there in prison it's just like a city, you know, a town. They have their movies every Sunday. The only way you can get to the movies is by having a privilege card. A privilege card is a card with your picture. When they take that privilege card away from you, it's because you've done something bad, and they take it away for say maybe one month or maybe two weeks. And then in the yards — the yards there were kind of small, and it was so crowded — you'd be playing dominoes, on the ground.

Another thing happened, but I didn't see it; this guy wasn't in my barracks. I just heard that a guy, when his time was up for him to leave, he killed a guy. And they sentenced him to the gas chamber for killing the guy there in prison. And he was about to leave. We used to talk about it a lot. They would say, "That guy was crazy. One week and he would have been out in the free world. And he gets into this kind of trouble."

In prison there are a lot of little gangs. These guys told me never to get into one of those little gangs, because you get into trouble. The old-timers that were there told me that. Because there used to be old-timers that had been there forty, fifty years. And I used to like to go over there by the old-timers and listen to stories about how they used to live in those days. About when they used to have stagecoaches, horses, and they used to run races and all that. Those guys used to get mad at each other because they used to say, "Oh, my horse was faster than yours," and all that. I used to love that, to listen to the old men.

I met a lot of buddies there, boys from San Bernardino that I used to hang around with. So then I didn't feel so lonesome because I knew some guys. One of those boys, he was a fighter there in prison, and he was champion of all the guys in prison. I used to hang around with these boys from San Bernardino and then we eat and afterwards we used to stay out in the sun and talk.

When I was there I was learning to be a mechanic. I can fix a little bit, but I didn't finish the course. I can fix any older models, but not the new ones. But older models, like '51 styles, I can fix. They had a lathe there, and I was trying to learn how to use it, for furniture legs, stuff like that. That's what I was doing. But I would like to learn to be a mechanic for cars, because I've done a little bit of it.

*   *   *

I remember one time in Watsonville there was a boy named Bob Maise. He used to work in the same cannery where I was, and he was fired. He had a car, a '51 Ford. And then he traded that Ford for a Chevie. One day he says to me that the Chevie needed fixing. He says, "You want to help me fix this car?" And I told him, "Oh, that's easy to fix." And he asked me, "What do you need to do, so it won't burn oil?" So I told him, "Why don't you put new rings on it?"

So he bought new rings, gaskets, and everything. And then I told him, "Well, you buy a set of socket wrenches, because we're going to need them." So finally we took that motor apart; we took everything apart, and I put rings on it. And then when we fixed it, everything was good.

But then the motor was too tight, you know. It wouldn't go. We had to push it with a car, to get it going. And it still wouldn't turn. The motor was too tight. And I told him, "Maybe you have to take the front off and loosen the bolts on the pistons." And he says, "No, maybe if we push it, it'll go." And I told him, "No, I don't think so. Maybe we try it with a crank." And it was too hard to turn it with a crank. So we went to a garage, and we put in a starter and then the parts turn, they start turning for maybe twenty minutes. Just turn, but it won't start. Pretty soon they got loose, I guess, and they start. And I thought it was going to be no good because it was too tight.

This boy, Bob Maise, he used to come, and we go to drive-ins and all that. From work we used to go to eat hamburgers, stuff like that. He used to buy me food a lot, so that's how come I helped him with his car. I didn't charge him anything. When I needed his car, he used to let me have it. He used to go to my house all the time. And then my brother come there in the afternoons, and we used to go around the town, just drive around the town, see the girls, whistle at them, and then stop. We'd say, "You want a ride?" Sometimes they would get in the car.

* * *

When I got out of San Quentin I got deported right away. They deported me to Tijuana again. As soon as I cross the border one policeman told me, "You back again?" "Yeah, I'm back." That was the last time I got into trouble. From then on I used to get in trouble just with the Immigration, about getting picked up, you know. But nothing that I had done wrong. Just for the Immigration.

7. Back and Forth Across the Border

I just kept jumping the border, you know, because I liked the States. I couldn't get used to living here in Mexico. Because I had never lived in Mexico, it seemed to me like I was in a country where you don't know nobody. Like they put you someplace where you don't know nobody, you are all isolated or something. I used to think of that. But finally I thought, Well, if I come to Mexico City, maybe I'll stay, because if I live close to the border I will jump. But now I think if I go near the border, I wouldn't jump. Now I got used to staying here in Mexico.

*   *   *

Most of the Immigration places are nice, just like a hotel. They give you everything. They have good meals, just like a restaurant. Sometimes in the morning you had cornflakes, hot cakes, bacon, and fried eggs. It's nice, but you are just like in jail. They take you out; they have playgrounds where you go out and play baseball, volley-ball, football.

Every day you get up around six o'clock in the morning. I used to take care of the kitchen, take care of washing the pots and pans. Then I used to get up at five o'clock in the morning, because you eat breakfast before the other guys that don't work, see. You eat breakfast and then the people come in and then you start serving them, like servants. Like if I was serving cornflakes, each man would pass you his bowl and you had to give him a little bit. Another would give the milk, like a cafeteria or a chow line in the army.

Then after breakfast, you would have about two hours where you don't do nothing. You would go out and just sit around and play cards, take it easy. Then when it was twelve o'clock — the regular meal that they have in the States, not like here where it is two o'clock — then you would go back, eat before they do. Then at suppertime it is the same way, the same routine. Then when it was all through, we had to clean the mess hall very good, clean it and wash the floors. Then we would go out and play for maybe one or two hours before they would call bedtime. Bedtime was around nine o'clock.

Before the lights would go out you would be doing little things, like anything you would like to make, recreation. Like a wallet you want to make, anything you can make out of string. That's where I learned how to make those woven doilies that I was making. There was another boy that was making them there. You just look, and they would tell you how it is made. I learned from some other Mexicans, other boys that were making them there. They didn't have no teachers. The only teachers there were for making wallets. I learned how to make wallets from an American teacher. You had to buy the leather, and then they would teach you how to make wallets. They don't give you no money at all, not like in that first camp where you could make maybe five, ten dollars a week in general construction.

These tattoos that I got, most of them were put on in the Immigration camps. The first tattoo I got when I was about eighteen years old. No, maybe less than that, around seventeen, when I made the first tattoo. I got that one in San Bernardino. I had it made in a little shop that they had there. I was just walking past by a tattoo place and was watching the tattoos and all of a sudden one boy said, "How would you like a tattoo on your hand?" "No, it hurts too much." "No," he says, "if you want it, I will pay for it." And I said, "No, it hurts too much." And he said, "Oh, don't be chicken." "OK, I will do it." Well, all three of us got one, and they paid for mine. It was on my hand, two hands crossing, shaking hands. And my father got mad; he hit me. Then after that I got another one in Fresno, on my arm.

These tattoos on my chest were put on in the Immigration camps, like San Pedro and El Centro. They are both in California. I just had them put on for the hell of it, you know. They had nothing to do, so lots of people put tattoos on. Even my wife asked me, "How come you let them put those tattoos on?" A lot of people have asked me, "Did they tie you to put them on?" A lot of people think that when they deport you across the border, the Immigration ties you up and marks you, but that isn't true. And I said, "No, they don't tie you like that."

Sometimes you stay in those camps a long time because there are a lot of people. They take some today, and then what they pick up today they can't put over right away, because they have some other guys to throw over the border first. If they don't have very many, they can put you over right away. Then you are turned over to the Mexican government, and they make a record that you have been deported, but they don't hold you or anything. The Mexican officials don't hold you, they just let you through. The American officials have a paper that they give to the Mexican Immigration. They just tell you, "OK, go back and don't cross the border no more." And sometimes the Mexicans tell you, "See, they don't like you there and still you are going back there," and all that bullshit, but you just don't pay no attention.

*   *   *

I remember when I was about twenty-eight and I was in the detention of the Immigration in San Pedro. There I met some people that were killing time there because they didn't want to go into the army. They were Americans, and they didn't want to go to the armed service because they had to go and kill somebody, and they didn't believe in it. They got sentenced for two years for refusing to go and fight in World War II.

You meet a lot of kinds of people in them camps, like people that forge checks and people that are smuggling. They smuggle marijuana or dope or cars through the border. They get caught, and they are put in those facilities there in San Pedro. A lot of them, they do a lot of time, five years for smuggling marijuana from Mexico into the States.

I knew lots of those guys. I knew one of them that was smuggling dope, you know. He was a Mexican, and he had a partner that was an American. I met them there, both of them. But the Mexican, he used to bring the dope to Tijuana at the border, and then he used to give it to the American, and the American used to bring it across the border and then bring it to Los Angeles.

And you know, when you get it, it is just like tar. You know how tar looks, black. And then when you cook it — that's the way they used to explain it to me — they cook it with sugar, and then they cut it into pieces, pieces like this, about an ounce. And they had quarters of an ounce, and then they used to sell it to girls and boys that had that habit. They would sell a little paper, maybe one gram, for a lot of money. And they did that for maybe five years. He told me that he had a lot of money, because in those five years he got a big ranch and everything.

But finally he got caught. He left his town in Mexico with four pounds of that stuff, and he says that when he got in the train he had a feeling that somebody was following him, but they didn't want to catch him until they caught his partner; they wanted to catch everybody. So he got to Tijuana and he gave it to this American boy, and because he had papers he crossed the border too. But they wanted to catch the whole band. So when they got to Los Angeles, and they got into this house, then right away the police circled the house and they caught everybody with, I think it was in retail price two million dollars that they had.

He used to tell all of those stories, how they got caught and all that. But he said another guy put the finger on them, that's how they got caught. They said that there are two kinds of habit — one that you get inside the skin, and one that you put in the veins. Once you get it in the veins you have to have it every day. And when you don't have it, you just go, like crazy. Yeah, you can kill your own mother just to get money to get dope.

I never tried it. But I know one boy that sold his mother's television and furniture just to buy that stuff. When the mother went home and she saw her house empty, she went to the cops and told that her son was an addict. And they picked him up and they took him to a hospital. In San Bernardino I have two cousins, a man and a girl, that are dope addicts. And this male cousin of mine, he went to the Mexican authorities to get cured. My aunt sent him there because he used to steal and rob just to get that stuff.

I never tried it, not even marijuana that they say is not so bad. All I do is drink, tequila, pulque; I tried all those. I even tried cactus juice, but I didn't try no marijuana. Marijuana is just like a cigarette, they say. I don't know, maybe you try it, you get to like it, you can't stay off of it. So I never tried it.

When we jumped the border, most of the time we go by night. We never jumped the border in the daytime. Every time it was in the night. You can't see, you know. You can't see, you go just on direction. And you figure, Los Angeles is in this direction, and you cross a mountain and come to another one. We would sleep out in the bushes. You have a jacket or something, and you just lay down there in the bushes. You bring food for a certain number of days. You figure, well, it's going to take three days, so you bring enough food and water. So you sleep under a tree there all day, until when it gets dark you start going again. That's how we used to do it. Most of the boys that jump the border go by night.

But sometimes you do it during the day, when you're way out where nobody can see you. But if you're in places where you are going to have to ask for directions, you never go by day, because if somebody sees you, they call the Immigration. Because that happened to me one time. One time we were hiding in an orchard, a grapefruit orchard, and then one man saw us. So we thought, well, maybe this man isn't going to say nothing. Pretty soon we see the Immigration coming. And he says, "OK, boys, let's go." And we thought that man wasn't going to tell them.

One time I crossed the border from Tijuana to go to Los Angeles. I had to walk from Tijuana clear to Los Angeles. I crossed the mountains; in the mountains we were very high, you know. I had to take about fourteen days to get to L.A. by crossing the mountains, because if you go by highway there would be a lot of Immigration officers.

This boy went with me, and he couldn't make it through the mountains, climbing the high mountains. You know how tired you get climbing, going down on another mountain, up and down. And this boy, he got so sick I thought he was going to die on me. I thought this boy was dying, and I didn't know what to do. He fainted from walking too much, and then I had to put water on him to bring him back, and then we rested for half a day. Pretty soon he was all right; he was just all pooped out, you know. Then we walked and we got to Orange County, from Tijuana to Orange County, which is about forty miles from Los Angeles. We got there, and from there we got a bus.

*   *   *

The Immigration doesn't beat you up. Lots of people have believed that the Immigration people beat you up, but the Immigration people in California treat you very nice. They don't beat you up. The Immigration people that really do beat you up and are very rough with you are the Immigration from Texas. Those will beat you up.

When somebody jumps the border, you know, the Immigration can know by your footprints. When you cross the border, there are the footprints, and they know a man crossed. But they don't follow you; they get an airplane, you know. They get an airplane, and they circle around, and they have a loudspeaker in the airplane.

One time that we jumped the border, we were resting under a tree. It was early in the morning, about six o'clock. And this airplane was circling, and there were a lot of fields. I thought that this airplane was the kind that puts that powder on the fields, you know, for dusting the crops. I thought he was dusting, so I didn't pay any attention. All of a sudden I heard, "Hombres, come out." In Spanish, you know. I told the boys, "Oh, it's the Immigration, you got to go out." I told these four guys, I said, "You guys go."

And they went out. I stayed there and hoped they wouldn't come for me. But when the airplane saw those guys going, on the loudspeaker he said, "There is one more." He says, "Hombre, come out." He was talking to me. And I stayed there; I didn't want to go out. And he stayed around. All day long he was in that airplane, you know. He would go and come back, go and come back. He would circle, and I was still there. It was during the daytime, and I thought, if I stay one more hour he won't catch me because it is getting dark. As soon as it got dark, I got out of there. And then I saw a little light. It probably wasn't anything, maybe Immigration, they burn a cigarette. And I saw the light, and I circled around them.

Another time when the Immigration caught me, they talked about this, how they caught some men with the plane, and there was another one there, but they couldn't get him to come out. And I told them that was me. They said, "We didn't want to go in there after you because we thought you might have a gun or something."

Then another time that we crossed from Mexicali we walked about fifty miles. Then we got a train, and these trains pass through a lot of towns where the Immigration inspect the train, you know. We stopped at one town in California, which is the center for Immigration, for them to inspect the train. When the train stopped there we had to get off, and everybody started running because there would be a lot of Immigration. When I seen the train slow down, I would jump from the train and hide someplace. Then when the train would start up again, we would hike the train again.

There were a lot of people that used to get on those boxcars where they put the ice. Then they would close the door, and sometimes they would jam the door, and then you can't open it. A lot of wetbacks died. They starved because they couldn't open the door. And a lot of those tanks, you know those oil tanks, a lot of people used to get into them, and they would suffocate. That's why I never used to get into those places. Sometimes we used to jump off the train, and we would lay around in the orchards. All we had for food was oranges and grapefruits. We used to have it rough, sometimes, jumping the border into the United States. I haven't tried it no more.

The last time I jumped the border, I stayed for about four years without getting picked up by the Immigration. Finally they picked me up in Santa Cruz, California. They picked me up and sent me to Santa Rita, and from Santa Rita they took me to San Francisco before the judge, and the judge sentence me to eighteen months for illegal entry. They send me to prison near San Pedro, California, to serve eighteen months. But I wrote to that judge, and the judge cut my time to six months, and five years on probation.

Ever since I haven't gone back to the United States. Because now I think it is better to be here in Mexico than to be running all the time when you see a cop or an Immigration officer. If I ever do go back, I think I would like to go with papers.

8. Work Experiences on Both Sides of the Border

The lowest wage pay that I ever got in the States was years ago, when I worked for Japanese. I got twenty-five cents an hour, twenty-five cents for working. That was about 1939, I think. I must have been around sixteen or seventeen. I hadn't quit school yet, but I used to work for them, part-time. That was the worst pay that I got in the States. The hardest job that I done was in a steel factory, where they melt steel. It comes out real red, real red, and that's a hard job. That's one of the hardest jobs I ever done in my life. The best pay that I got in the States was when I used to work loading lettuce at eight cents a crate. I remember when we used to make sometimes forty dollars, fifty dollars a day. That was the job I used to like best in the United States, working in the lettuce with my brother David. We used to cut the lettuce and pack it, and we used to load it in big trucks. It was a good job.

There was another time that I worked in Los Angeles picking up garbage cans they put in front of the house; picking up garbage with a truck. And then we used to go inside the house to take their garbage, and they give you maybe fifty cents, twenty-five cents, for going in. I've done that in L.A. County. That was a good job, too. That paid good. I made $25 a day plus tips. In a week, probably around $140. It was good!

One time I was a truck driver in Mexico, hauling corn and wheat. It was a good job, but it didn't pay too much. I usually only made 270 pesos a month, which is not very good pay. So I decided to look for a better job, so I went to lower California. There I worked as a tractor driver, plowing the grounds. And then when I worked there I used to work picking cotton, working in the onions, lettuce.

And I used to work in the strawberries, too, in the States. Apples and peas, too. And then I remember one time that I worked in California picking lemons there. When I wasn't working, during the nights, I used to go out, have a nice time with a girl named Charlotte. She was nice, and I used to go around with her. I thought I was going to get married with her, but it was just a girl, just another girl that I never took very seriously.

When I was working with the oranges, picking fruit, then I moved from one place to another a lot. See, the people follow the fruit in California. Say you're picking oranges in San Bernardino, well, maybe several hundred miles away is another crop, so we go there. Like say they have lettuce in Salinas Valley — the lettuce they have is good there, you know. Pretty soon the lettuce is finished and you go from Salinas to King City. That's only about maybe ninety miles. You come back every day. Then when the lettuce finishes in California, you probably move to Arizona. You come to pick lettuce in Phoenix, to pack lettuce. I never used to pack the lettuce. I used to nail the lids on the crates. And load lettuce on those big trucks, like those that carry beer — trailer trucks. We used to put lettuce inside, and then they take the lettuce to Los Angeles and the big cities.

And I used to work in cotton, just barely making enough. And then in the winter I got sick. I had a boil on my ankle, and I couldn't walk. And I used to lay in my room, nobody to take care of me. So finally this girl came to see me. I never used to come out, so she knocked on my door and asked me, "What's wrong?" I said, "I have a boil, I can't walk." And she says, "Oh, I'll cure you." So she washed it real good with water, hot water, and then she put a patch with salt pork, and that patch took everything out of my boil and cured me. And naturally I really appreciated her for curing my boil, and for gratitude I used to give her money. I used to give her presents for doing that. Finally this girl got married, and when I used to see her I used to tell her husband what she did for me.

Then another job I had was in Hollister, topping sugar beets with a long knife. The knife is long like a machete, but with a hook on the end. You hook the sugar beets, and cut all the leaves off. You work from six in the morning clear to five. And then you have to load the trucks so that, you know, it's a very hard day. I was twenty-two. My father was already here in Mexico, and my brother, he was someplace else.

I think my brother was in a town with his godmother in Reedley, California. That's a town where they farm nothing but grapes. He was living there with his godmother. Her husband died already. Her husband was old, you know, and real fat, so he died from a heart attack. They say he was too fat.

*   *   *

Once I used to work for a German, picking peaches. He had peaches and grapes. There used to be a lot of girls there to pack peaches, you know. And then this man was going to receive a whole bunch of nationals from Mexico to work his farm. He told me, "You want to be the foreman of these boys, you stay here." Because I spoke English and Spanish. And I said OK. So I stayed there, and when a bunch of wetbacks was coming we went to Fresno to receive these boys. And all the girls were there to receive them, and we had a dance for them. A dance and a big meal, a big celebration that they used to give for them boys, in them times. And I stayed there working for this German. He used to pay me twelve dollars a day when I was working for him.

Then me and one of those nationals got in a little argument, so I left this German guy, and went to another town. See, this national wasn't speaking English, and I was teaching him English. Once he learned to speak English he thought he was a better man, and he wanted to be the foreman and all that. So pretty soon he starts talking to this German guy to give him the job. So one day he started drinking beer, and he got mad over that job, so I hit this Mexican, and then I took off. I didn't want the job anyway, so I let him have it.

I left and worked at that kind of grass . . . they thrash it and they make paper out of it. They put it in bales, and we used to load them in trucks and send them to different parts. Then I used to go back every weekend to see my girlfriend that I had in this other town. Once I brought one boy with me, but he tried to take this girl away from me.

He told this girl, "Why do you go around with him, he's not your kind. He hasn't got no money. I have a lot of money, a car, and a house." So I told the girl, "If you love him you can go with who you want to." She said, "No, I don't love him, I love you, I don't want him. The only thing I tell you, what kind of friends do you have that try to take your girlfriend away?" "Well," I says, "I didn't know he was that kind, so I am never going to bring him no more." And then he used to come by himself. Yeah, try to take the girl away from me. And she used to tell me, "Your friend came over and was blowing the horn for me to come out, but I didn't go out." I never had a fight with him because I didn't care, you know. I didn't think that he would take her away. If he would have taken her away, probably we would have had a little discussion about that, but I never got to be in a fight with him.

Another time I went to work in a town near Los Angeles. I lived in Santa Paula forty or fifty miles from San Fernando. We used to have a car, and about five or six guys would drive every day a distance of fifty or sixty miles. We worked in construction; we were making ditches for sewer pipes. Pretty soon I got tired of going back and forth, so I talked to another uncle of mine that lived in Santa Paula by the name of Aurelio Jiménez. He was a first cousin of my mother's.

And I talked to him and he told me that I could come pick lemons in Santa Paula, because one of his brothers was a foreman in citrus. But I didn't know how to pick lemons. Because you have a range, you have to know the size of the lemon, the color, and everything. So finally he taught me how to pick lemons. After that I got pretty good and he told me, "You like to work loading lemons?" I said OK, because it was pretty easy; only the lemons were heavy, not like oranges. You have to stack them six high, and that was hard work. I stayed there for quite a while in Santa Paula. Then my brother came to Santa Paula and he stayed there for a little while. Then they call him for the draft, and he went to the army.

I think it was 1946. World War II. He was drafted and taken to Texas, and then I moved from Santa Paula to Gilroy. I was working in the fields there. And all of a sudden one day — I was kind of by a bar — I saw a soldier coming down the street, and I told one boy, "That looks like my brother." And then as he got closer, he was my brother. "How come you are on leave?" And he said, "I am going overseas." And I said, "When are you going to leave?" "From San Francisco on the 28th."

He stayed there for a little while then. Pretty soon I said, "Don't you have to go?" He said, "No," and he stayed there for about nine more days, and his boat left, so he didn't go. And then a few days later he left; he went back, and they put him on another boat, and he went to his same company that was already in Tokyo. He stayed there; he worked as a lineman, putting in telephone poles. There was still a little band of guerillas, Japanese, you know, who hadn't given up. He says that Tokyo was all teared down from the war and all that. He told me all about it. He came back from Tokyo to California. I think he stayed two years and a half.

When he came back, I wasn't in California no more. I was in Oregon. And he went to look for me, he went to look for me in Oregon. The name of the town was Eugene, I think it was.

I went to Oregon because a lot of people were talking about making money in the lumber business, so we signed up for the lumber. And we went there, and all the boys got a job. I got me a good job, hauling the logs with a caterpillar. And the other guys got their jobs sawing by hand. And they quit right away, because it was too tough a job.

I was there for six months. Every Saturday we used to go to Eugene. All the loggers would work for the week, and then they would go spend their money in the bars, raising hell. Then they would look for some girls. You know, you drink in the bars and pretty soon you are drunk, and you spent all your money, and you have to work all over again. I used to spend my money just like any of them, drinking with girls. At first I didn't want to drink with them girls, but they told me, "Aw, you don't know what living is like." So finally I gave in, and I started doing the same thing that they did. But I got tired of that, and I told the boss I was going to leave. He said, "Don't leave, this is a good job." "Yeah, this is a good job, but this drinking I don't like, I have to take off." So I took off.

*   *   *

Right after my brother was drafted I ended up in Tijuana, so I stayed there during that time right after the war. There was a lot going on in Tijuana. I met a lady there, and she told me to come to work for her. And she told me she would pay me good; she would pay me fifteen dollars a day. That's a good job, fifteen dollars, for working in Mexico. So I said, "OK, I'll be there tonight."

And then I started working there, and she told me, "All you have to do is just watch, and if somebody comes, you have to let me know." And I says OK. For a few days I didn't know what was going on. I used to watch in front, and a lot of people used to come in through the back. So finally one day I got kind of curious, "What kind of job this is? I only stay here watching in case somebody comes." "Watch if the policeman comes," she told me. She would give me one day off, and she would pay me.

So one day that I wasn't going to work I went to see what was going on. I went and I saw a lot of girls, and then I knew what it was, what kind of house it was. It was a house for American soldiers; they used to come in there, get a good time. Then if they liked the girl, they used to take her, you know. So this lady saw me, and she told me, "I didn't want you to know about it because I didn't think you would like to work for this kind of job." So I tell her, "Well, I'm not going to watch for cops no more, but I'll go to the border and bring the soldiers, and you give me one dollar for each soldier."

See, this one boy had told me, "You know how you can make some money?" I says, "How?" "You go to the border and all the army men, they come in, they come here looking for girls. You come in and get five or six of them, and you take them to this house, and this woman gonna give you a dollar for each guy."

So I went to the border. Soon I seen about ten of them coming all in a bunch, you know. And then I told them, "You like to have some fun?" And they said, "Yes, you know some good places to go?" And I took them to this place. Right away this lady give me the ten dollars, you know. And I said to myself, "This is good here."

So that night, you know how much I made? About $150. The lady used to give me one dollar for each. But I didn't know that it was against the law to do that. The Mexican police put you in jail. And then the guys used to give me sometimes five, ten dollars, you know, to show them a place. See, they used to tell me, "How much you going to charge to take us there?" I says, "You can give me whatever you want."

I made quite a bit. Even in the States you can't make this kind of money. But this money is no good because you make it too easy; you throw it away. Spend it drinking and all that, and on girls. And then I got tired of that kind of job. Then I start going to all the nightclubs in Tijuana. I used to dress real good. I didn't buy the clothes made. I go to a tailor and I tell him to make me a suit this way. I used to dress real good.

Then the cops in Tijuana used to see me there all dressed up, and then they say, "Where does this boy work? Where does he have a job or something?" So finally they used to keep an eye on me. And one man told me, "You've got to find you a job in case they going to ask you where you work." So I went and talked to one man: "You're a contractor here. I want you to give me a job just for a little while here in the mornings." And then I used to work there. "What am I going to pay you for the work?" "Just let me help you here. And you just give me something to eat," I told him. And I didn't eat nothing because in case a cop stop me I wanted him to tell him I worked for him, you know.

So that same day, I just got off his place working. I went in and washed, and then I got dressed, ready for night. Because everything in Tijuana starts around four o'clock in the afternoon. Everything is good then. This cop, this plainclothesman asked me, "Where are you working?" I says, "I'm working with this man over here." "Can you prove it?" I told him, "Yes, let's go and talk to him." He asked the man, "This man working for you?" And he told him, "Yes." So he let me alone. They would probably have put me in jail for fifteen days. That was not really a job, that was just . . . I did that for about six months.

I used to do that all the time and then go around the nightclubs. The girls from the nightclubs go and sit at the tables. And one day the announcer wasn't there. So this girl asked me, "Why don't you announce the floor show in this nightclub?" I says, "Yes, but it's not the same, speaking English in front of a microphone. I don't know how to say it. If I had a paper where it is written down the things I'm going to say, then I could go." Then she went and brought me a list, you know, how the girls are coming out, to announce their floor show. And then she wrote down some jokes in English, and I used to read those jokes out through a microphone to all the tourists and navy guys. They laugh and all that. So finally they told me to stay, to be the announcer there. "I don't like this job, I do better what I do," I tell the girls.

So this girl asks, "While you're announcing, you come and live with me." This girl she used to dance a striptease. She would come out there and take everything off piece by piece, until she had nothing at all. I used to announce that. Actually, they don't take everything off. They leave a little . . . really thin, just like the color of their skin. I used to see. I lived with her there. And then I told her, "Well, I think it's about time for me to go some place, to change places, because the cops here in Tijuana just keep looking at me, when I go out." Then I left Tijuana and went to Enseñada.

*   *   *

Enseñada is only about fifteen miles from Tijuana. Enseñada is a tourist town, on the Mexican side. I went there, and I stayed there for a little while. And there was nothing doing there in that town, so I left. And I came back to Tijuana. In Tijuana I bought a ticket to go to Tecate. And there I stayed for just a little while. Then I came to Mexicali, and I jumped the border. I came all the way to San Jose, by myself on the bus. And then I got me a job in a big cannery. I made darn good money there, and I bought me a Chevie, on time, you know.

Then one man that was working there, he told me, "If you would go to the border and bring back some relatives of mine that are waiting there, they want to come, I will pay you good if you go bring them." And I told him, "How much you going to pay me if I go bring them?" He says, "I give you one hundred dollars for each guy." There was four of his relatives. And I told him, "OK, I'll go."

So I went, you know. And I cross into Mexicali, and then I went and looked for these guys, and I told them that their relative in San Jose had told me to come and pick them up. And I told them, "Get ready to leave about nine o'clock tonight." And they all got ready and got in the car, and then we came close to the border. At that time there was no fence. It was easy to cross the border. So we drove the car through. We drove the car about one mile outside of the town, then we crossed the border, and then we came all the way to San Jose. All that way that we came in the car we didn't see no Immigration officers or nothing. So we got there. Then I brought them right to this man, and he gave me four hundred dollars.

So these men tell me, "You know what? There's four more girls over there that you should have brought." I says, "Oh, I didn't know, these guys didn't tell me anything." "Would you like to go for these four girls?" I said, "Yes, but you've got to give me fifty dollars in advance for each one. Then I go." Because I wanted to pay off the car, you know, that's why I went. So I went back to Mexicali, and

I found these girls, and then we cross the same way, and we came all the way.

Then my brother was mad when I got to San Jose. He says, "Don't do that no more because you don't have no papers and they're going to get you. They get the car too and everything." So I say, "Yeah." So I didn't go no more. Then the same man asked me, "How come you don't go and get a friend of mine that's over there?" "No, no more. Because the Immigration is too tough right now. Because I heard that an uncle of mine went and he got caught at the border, and they fined him ten thousand dollars." So I paid off my car doing that, but then I didn't go no more.

Around that time I went to live with another uncle of mine named José Hernández. He was my mother's brother, and he had six children. He and his wife Angela made eight, and I was nine. His house was really well furnished, because all his sons used to work picking nuts. They'd shake the tree, and the nuts fall down and they pick them up. Walnuts. They used to make five hundred dollars a week, total. He had four daughters and two sons, and all the family used to pick the nuts.

So they had their house in really good condition. The house belonged to them. They had very expensive furniture. Like in the living room they used to have two sofas and two chairs, television; and they had their television in one of those long record players, those big ones. What do you call them? Consoles. And they had another room, they call it a study room, you know. When the smaller children used to go to school, they used to do their homework there in that room. And then when you come to read books or magazines, you sit down there and read them. And then they had a big kitchen. Their house was nice.

I was working in picking pears and apricots when I was there. Pears and apricots, that's all they plant there. See, you pick the apricots when they are not really ripe, but between ripe and green. And the pears you pick them green, because they ship them to some other place, and they get ripe on the way. I must have been around twenty-five or a little older when I lived there. My uncle was good to me, but the only thing, he want you to dress like an old-timer. He didn't want you to get dressed like the youth.

See, at that time there was a lot of *pachucos*. That's what they used to call them in the States — Mexicans who used to dress with their pants real baggy, you know. And then their shoes used to be real thick, maybe three soles to make them high. And my uncle didn't like all that. And he didn't like nobody to wear their hair long. Because one time I remember I went there, he took me straight to the barbership, and then they cut all my hair.

I wore the clothes, but I never belonged to no gangs of pachucos. I just used to dress like them, but I never belong to none of those pachuco gangs. The girls, they used to dress like pachucos, too; they used to wear their dresses high, about maybe four inches above the knee. My uncle didn't like all that, and he used to say, "Why don't you dress a little decent?" And I told him, "I haven't got any other clothes." And then he gave me some of those clothes, long old-timer clothes, you know, that he used to wear way back. With the bottom really wide, you know. And the pachucos used to wear them almost tight to your ankles, but like balloons on the tops.

Finally the Immigration caught me in a cantina there one night, and I got deported. Then I was in Mexico again, and I came to Mexico City because they were going to send some men to the United States as braceros. So I came, and there were thousands of people waiting there to get jobs as braceros. Oh, I thought, I would never get there because there were thousands. So finally one man told me, "You want to go as a bracero?" I said, "Yes." "Well, I will sell you a pass to get in." I said, "How much you want for that pass?" "Well," he said, "give me one hundred pesos." So I said OK. So I gave him a hundred pesos for the pass, and I got in to see the doctor for a physical check and everything. Finally we pass all that physical checking, and they said, "Well, a certain day, you all are going to leave." So they told us to be in the railroad station at a certain time. And we all got in the train; it was about six or seven cars of all braceros. I was the only one who could speak English.

And when the train came, when the train cross the border, they had to get your name and everything. They had your papers, and everything was clear. We crossed the border, and they brought us all the way, on the train, all the way to Fresno, California. There in Fresno there was a lot of ranchers. They would give, say, fifty dollars for fifty guys. And then one rancher asked, "Any of you guys speak English?" So I said, "Yes, a little." "Well, I want you to pick out fifty of the best you think are good workers." So I told him, "OK," so

I picked out most of the guys that came from the town that I was born in, and we went to work for him.

The rancher told me, "You're going to be my foreman." I says, "I don't like to be foreman because these men, I tell them what to do, then they get mad." "No, you're going to get better pay than they do; you be my foreman." I says OK. So he teach me how to prune trees, and then I had to tell the men how to prune the trees. And after that, when something was wrong, they would tell me, "Well, you tell the boss!"

* * *

Another time I came to Mexico and I lived here a while and I met some soldiers who said, "Do you want to join the Mexican army?" Finally one day I decided, Oh, I'll join the Mexican army. And I got in, and I joined the Mexican army. And they sent us to Puebla. We all had to train for three months, and then after three months they gather you in, they have your name, and then you have to swear to the flag. I was supposed to stay three years in the Mexican army, but I didn't stay. We used to guard the trains, the passenger trains. Like a policeman, but we were soldiers.

And then one time, we had to guard the payroll car, you know, payroll for the soldiers. We went to a little town with the Indians there, you know, Mexican Indians. They are mean. They didn't like soldiers; they used to kill the soldiers. I forget the name of the town, but it is in the state of Puebla. I think they were Toltec Indians, the Toltecas. And we stayed there, and one guy, one soldier that was with us, he got down off the train to go get a bottle, and he didn't come back. The lieutenant told him not to get off because they would probably kill him or something. He didn't show up. Next day we found out that he was dead. Somebody stabbed him.

Nobody likes the soldiers because they say a soldier is one of the lowest . . . like they say a soldier smokes marijuana and all that. That's why a lot of people don't like them. So one day finally I get tired, and so I take off. I stayed in the army about six months. And I was supposed to stay three years, but I take off. So I took off in Mexico City, and I took a train to my father.

I went and told my father, and my father says, "They are going to come and look for you here because they know you are from here." So I told him, "I'll go to the United States then." My father says,

"Well, I will go with you," and my father came with me, and we took the train to Guadalajara, and from Guadalajara we transferred to a bus.

We took a bus to go toward Mexicali. There was an old dirt road, you know. And then that bus breaks down in the middle of the desert. And all the people that was in the bus had to get under trees or under the bus or something, because it was very hot out. And me and some other guys, we walked clear to the next town. My father stayed out there where the bus was broken down. And we walked to the town to tell them to come and fix the bus. So they came and fixed the bus, and then we got the train to Mexicali.

My father went to work with my uncle on a ranch near Mexicali, in the cottonfields, and I went to work also. And my father met a woman, a girl; she had three children. She was a young girl, but she had three children already, small ones. And she lived with my father until first Edward was born to this lady, and then Lita was born, and then two more. They are all half sisters and half brothers of mine. Two girls and two boys. But my stepmother died while she was going to have Lupe, she died of that, of childbirth. He didn't get married to her, he just lived with her. Those children that she had before she lived with my father, they are not related to me. She already had those. My father never knew who the first one was before he got with her.

After a while there in Mexicali, I jumped the border again. The army went to look for me that day, but I wasn't in Mexicali anymore. They didn't look for me after that. After a certain year they don't look for you no more. I never changed my name, because here is not like in the States. See, in the States, you desert, they really get after you, but they don't get after you like that here in Mexico. Here they only train for in case of war. In the States it's more serious when you get into uniform. Mexico doesn't have any wars, only revolutions, and they fight among each other.

In the Mexican army nothing happened, you know. And then you had to buy your own clothes, buy your own food. They don't give you the food free like in the States. They pay you 2½ pesos every day so you can buy your meals. One boy there, he used to get the rifle and point it right at you, and stuff like that. And I used to get that rifle, and, boy, did I give it to him. They used to call him

Enchocolate, because he was very dark. He used to load one rifle and I load another one and we play with each other like that, pointing them at each other. That's one of the worst incidents I can remember.

*   *   *

Around then my brother was living in Watsonville. That's where he met his wife. His wife was going to school, to high school. She was around fourteen years old. And I guess they fell in love, so he took his wife with him when he moved. They went to San Bernardino, and they lived in San Bernardino for six months. She was under age, you know; she was only fourteen years old. My brother was twenty-two, I think.

They were looking for her, and finally they caught up with them. They found out where they were. The cops took my brother and the girl and threw my brother in jail. The mother of the girl came for her and brought her to Watsonville. And then they took my brother to Watsonville, and they asked him, "How come you never married her?" and all that. And finally they sentenced him to six months. After the six months were up, he had to marry her, because she was under age and she was already pregnant. So he married her; he married this half-Filipino girl.

He wrote to me that he had to marry this girl and that he was in jail. And I told him, "I'm sorry, but I can't go see you in jail, because maybe there's some Immigration there that will catch me." I was in a town not very far from there, about fifty miles from where he was in jail. I used to write to him, and I used to go see his wife, and give her a carton of cigarettes to take to him. I sent them money to help them a little bit. Because, you know, he always helped me.

Right now, I don't know where he is. The last time I heard, he was in Arizona. I think my younger half sister knows, but she doesn't tell me. That sister of mine, she's just that way. Because she thinks I would try to find out where he is and write to him and meet him. She wants me to stay here in Mexico, out of trouble!

My brother had three daughters. They were very happy for a while. And then his wife decided to have herself operated on, so she wouldn't have no more babies. And I told her, "Well, if you have an operation, I think you and my brother is going to be separated." So she says, "No, I don't think so." She went to a hospital and had herself operated on so she wouldn't have no more babies.

After four months they had separated. My brother said that she was no good no more. She had no feelings or nothing like that, see. You know, like when your feelings are there, making love, like that. You don't . . . it's not the same no more, like she wasn't the same, as my brother used to say. She wasn't the same woman like before. So they got separated. And my brother got out of the house and left everything, all the furniture and everything he had for her and for the children. He only took the car, and he left.

They never lived together again. They are still separated. Last time I heard he was over in Arizona. My brother said one time that he didn't want to go to California because they probably pick him up, put him in jail for nonsupport, you know. I told him he should send her some money.

I only have contact with my niece, my niece that goes to high school. She writes to me all the time, my brother's daughter. The other day she sent me a photograph of her.

I used to live with my brother. Sometimes my brother used to go out, and my sister-in-law and I'd stay home. But there was a girl there that used to take care of my brother's kids, a young girl. I used to tell my brother, "Don't leave this girl here! I can stay by myself. This girl could sometime maybe attack me!" Because I think, well, I'm here by myself, and this girl is here in the house. One of these days you might feel like you might want to do something. So I tell him, "Don't keep her in the house." The girl was around nineteen years old and nice. She used to wear her things real tight, and she liked to fool around. And she fooled around, and then she got a baby from some other guy. And then afterwards, when she had the baby, she wanted me to marry her. And I said, "No, never."

I used to help my brother dress his children, because they were so much in debt. They used to owe too much, like they had a television on time, and their refrigerator and most of the furniture they had was on time. Week after week they would have nothing left over, so I used to buy clothes for the children, like shoes, dresses, and everything. Most of the time I spent quite a bit of my money on them. A lot of money, because I used to make quite a bit. Almost every month I used to buy them shoes, or a dress, like that. That's how come I never saved no money. Once in a while I used to send money through to my father, here in Mexico.

In Watsonville, when I lived with my brother, we rented a whole house, a nice house. And then we used to have a lot of furniture. Like we had two televisions, a telephone, a sofa, some chairs, and another sofa that would go into a bed. And then we had three bedrooms with bedroom sets. It takes quite a bit of money to furnish a house like that. And then in the dining room we had the dining table, with all the chairs. Good chairs! We paid eighty dollars a month for the house. I was living with my brother, but most of the furniture, I bought it. My sister-in-law is still in Watsonville, but not in the same house. I guess she still has that furniture, but maybe she traded it or sold it and bought some other ones.

*   *   *

Before I lived with my brother, one time I worked in a town named Santa Ana. I was working there for Japanese people, out in the fields picking squash, string beans, and peas. I must have been around thirty. And there used to be a man there that was a Protestant. A Mexican, born in the States. And he asked me, would I like to go to his church? And I told him I was a Catholic. He says, "Well, you can come to my church; maybe you will change from a Catholic to a Protestant." I told him, "I don't think so because they say that Protestants have to get baptized and all that." "Well, come anyway."

So I went and listened. They were interested in me right away. They called themselves brothers, *hermanos*. You know how churches are, they are all brothers. It was a Pentecostal church. I went there for quite a while, all the time I was working there. Pretty soon they told me, "There is a girl here that you talk to very much." And they thought she was my girl. "Would you like to marry this girl? You can marry this girl, and we will pay all expenses." And they used to ask me, "Do you have any clothes?" I says, "No, I don't have any." "Well, if you like, we can buy you some and we will pay for them so you can go to church." They were like buying you to go to their church! "No," I said, "I don't need anything, I am working." Pretty soon I stopped going to the Protestant church.

I stopped going because I met another man who was a Christian Scientist. The Christian Scientists don't go to doctors or nothing like that when they are sick. They pray on their belief. Well, I started to listen to that man, and soon I started going to his church. The Christian Scientist church is not like a church. It is just a little place where they gather to talk, but it is too high for me to understand. The words are too tough for me to understand. But they used to explain to me what they believed. They didn't believe in doctors or medicine or nothing. They just believed in themselves, you know, that they can get cured by themselves. I only went about two times.

But in the Pentecostal church, they have, not a priest, what you call a pastor. He starts praying — not praying, but reading out of a bible, like chapter Saint Luke, chapter Saint so-and-so. We all had to sing a lot of songs. I don't remember the words. We'd just sing and pray. They don't get excited in the Christian Science church, but they get excited in this other church!

I went into the Holy Rollers church one time. And a person had a heart attack, and he fell down, and all the people say, "Don't touch him, the spirit has gone into him!" And then he was rolling all over the floor, biting his tongue. And the pastor said, "Don't touch him, the spirit has gone into him!" I went to the Holy Rollers because a friend invited me to go one day. Because you know, sometimes they are out in the streets telling you to go visit their churches, giving you little cards. And this guy had the heart attack. He had like a fit. The others were clapping their hands. Most of the people there were Mexicans and Negroes. The pastor was a Negro.

I was about to change one time to be a Protestant. In Santa Ana they told me that if you wanted to get baptized, they will baptize you, and they dress you all in white. I told them, "Well, I like your church, I will be a Protestant." "Okay, next Sunday you and two other boys will be baptized in the river." In the Santa Ana River. We were going to go, but just as we got up to it, I changed my mind. Well, I didn't like it, to be baptized in a river. You go right in the water, and then they get water and put it over your head, and then you are baptized. I got baptized as a Catholic here in Mexico. I was a baby, but I have the papers that say I was baptized.

*   *   *

In the 1950s when I lived with my brother, that's when I worked in Great West Frozen Foods. And I worked there for four years, and the boss there was real nice. I forget the name, but that boss there, he never bothered you. One boss, he was a Chinese, and another one was an American, and the general manager was Molly; they called him Molly. And another one that used to do the repack, he was a Mexican. His first name was Charlie. All the bosses were satisfied with me. I never was laid off. Other people, they would get laid off, but to me those bosses were nice. And a guy named Sancho, he told the bosses I was doing a nice job, and maybe that's why I was treated real nice. Sancho was just like a foreman, but he was a foreman in a warehouse where they have all these cardboards. Like boxes of cardboards that they used to pack all the frozen foods inside. They used to paint the name of the factory where it was going. We used to pack for a lot of big companies. Those boys were real nice.

I worked there in repack. The repack is where they have these little boxes already frozen; you get them and you put them in cases. Then they ship them to different parts of the United States or maybe Europe or someplace. I was the foreman there in the repack. And I used to work the day shift and sometimes the night shift. I had a good job there in Watsonville. I used to get $1.80 an hour. I was making good money there.

During those years when I wasn't working in the frozen foods I got a job with an uncle of mine. I used to work with him in a pool hall. You know how you fix the cue balls. And then he had a card game also in the pool hall, and I used to run the card game. Played poker there.

And one day the Immigration came in the pool hall, and when I saw the Immigration I put the cards down, and I went back of the bar like I was a bartender. Then that Immigration, he came in there and asked all the boys for their papers. And lots of boys didn't have papers. He took them out and put them in like a police truck. When they were in there I came outside, and I asked one of the Immigration, "Where are you taking those guys?" "Back to Mexico. Do you want to go with them?" And I said, "No, why should I go there? I would like to go for a visit sometime, but I was born here in the States."

Finally the Immigration caught me in 1958. They caught me, and they threw me over the border. In Watsonville they caught me. All that time I used to work, and I never used to go out very much because I didn't want the Immigration to catch me. So I used to give money to those three nieces that I have, the children of my brother, named Paula, Sharon, and another named Lee.

I didn't have no children until they deported me back to Tijuana. Then from Tijuana I went to Mexicali, and in Mexicali, that's where I met this girl. I didn't get married with her, I just lived with her. When she was pregnant, about three months before she had the baby, I decided to jump the border again. I stayed in Mexicali about six months, living with that girl there. I worked there picking cotton. That's all the kind of work they have in Mexicali, picking cotton. And then I jumped the border from Mexicali. I jumped the fence, because there really is a fence there!

And then I bought a ticket to San Bernardino, and I stayed there picking oranges. And then after that my brother came to San Bernardino to take me back to Watsonville. But then I didn't go to live in Watsonville; I just went there for a few days. I said, "I don't want to live here in Watsonville because the cops already know me. They might pick me up." "Well," he said, "let's move to San Jose." And then we moved to San Jose near San Francisco.

He moved with me because he was already going to move there. And so we moved to San Jose, and I got me a job in a cannery there, driving a forklift. I drove one of those forklifts, unloading boxes of tomatoes or peaches or pears. I worked there for quite a while. Then from that town, I used to work in different cities.

Like in Hayward. What do you call it where they have a lot of flowers? A nursery. Pruning the flowers, taking care of the flowers — that was a good job. We had to keep them inside so they wouldn't freeze. We used to cut them and put them out front and ship them to different places. I stayed around there for another four years before the Immigration caught me again.

In San Francisco one time around then they were signing up to go to work in Alaska, fishing in Alaska. I signed up, and I went to Ketchikan, Alaska. It's a fishing city, and I worked there on the schedule that I signed up for — three months. We went fishing on boats. I worked in a salmon boat, catching those salmon. And in three months we made a little over three thousand dollars. We made three thousand dollars, but in Alaska it is very expensive to live. Everything is very expensive in Alaska. You can make five or six thousand dollars, and you spend half of that for eating, because the food is very expensive. The place where we used to stay when we was not out on the water, in Ketchikan, you had to pay like twenty-five dollars for meals every day! Everything is expensive. I don't know how expensive it would be now, but everything was very expensive in them days.

When we got there it was very cold; we didn't see the sun. As soon as I got there I thought, "Oh, I go back, no sun!" Then we bought some sheepskin clothes, and that helped, so we stayed there for a while. When the three months was over we came back to the States.

We went back to San Francisco, and then I got a ticket to Seattle, by train. I worked there as a longshoreman for about three months. I worked with the longshoremen in Frisco, too. I used to work in the day, and then every night I used to go to a bar where a famous baseball player is the owner.

And they had a Mexican restaurant there in San Francisco called Panchito's. They used to call it by that name, and we used to go there to eat. I used to go there very often because I knew a girl there, and I wanted to make her. I used to go there every day, and pretty soon I started taking her to the beach in San Francisco. In San Francisco they have a beach, and they have a playground where they have like a carnival, and we used to get on the roller coaster. Later we began horse riding in San Francisco in the Golden Gate Park. Then this girl had to go back to New York. She left for New York, and I said I would go to see her some day, but I never got to see her. I knew her for a few months and then she went back.

That time around San Francisco was my last time in the States. I was maybe forty-one when I got deported, and I came to Mexico City. We came on the train, and I came direct to Mexico City, and then I looked for an aunt of mine, my father's sister, name of Lupe, Guadalupe. I looked her up, and I told her that I was deported. She said, "Don't go back to the States no more, you have been deported too many times. The next time they will probably put you in jail." So I said, "Okay, I won't go back there no more."

9. Mexico, Marriage, and Future Plans

You know, after I told my Aunt Guadalupe I wouldn't jump the border no more, I stayed there in Mexico City with her because I didn't have no job. So I took pictures, you know, photographs. I had them developed for maybe two pesos in Mexico City, and I used to resell them for maybe six pesos, whatever I could get. Like I take a photograph of you and develop it, and I take it to you and I sell it to you for a price. I worked at that for about six months, but I didn't like that, because we used to get tired, walking all the time. Like a postman, walking door to door.

Then I got a job in a moving van, one of those vans that move furniture from one place to another. We used to move furniture from Mexico City to Guadalajara, Monterrey, places like that. That job was pretty good, but I didn't like it. You had to sleep out on the highway in the truck. I had to help drive, too. And then afterwards when you are free all the boys would say, "Let's go to a cantina and get drunk." And I didn't like that. But we would all go to a cantina and drink. Drink beer, you know, and then we used to go to places where they had girls to entertain. This was in Monterrey.

In one of those places the girls weren't girls though. They were men dressed in women's clothes. But, like if you would go there, you would think they were girls by looking at them. One boy told me, "Why don't you dance with this girl?" And I said OK. I wanted to dance with her because she was really beautiful, just like a girl. And I asked her, "Would you like to dance?" And I started dancing with her, and everybody was laughing that I was dancing with her. "Why are they laughing?" I said.

And then we came and had a drink, and I invited her upstairs, you know. She wanted a drink. And then pretty soon she told me, "I am going to tell you something because you don't know. I am not a girl like you think. I am a man. But my feelings are just like a

girl. I dress like a girl. Everything is just like a girl, but I am a man."
I said, "Really?" He said "Yes." I said, "I don't believe you." He
said, "You can ask your friends over there."

And that was sure a surprise for me. I thought she was a girl.
She was really beautiful, and I thought maybe we could be friends,
and I could take her out to different places. And then afterwards she
told me she was not a girl but a man. So then my whole plan fell down
about me trying to get acquainted with her, for she was not a girl
after all, she was a man!

So I got real mad with my buddies, and I told them how cruel
they were in letting me talk to and dance with this man, a man that
was dressed in a woman's clothes. But they just laughed and told me
that they were playing a joke on me. Before it got too far they would
tell me that she was not a woman but a man. So my buddy told me,
"Well, let's go to another place where we can see some girls."

So we went to another place, and there were a lot of girls. I
didn't want to talk to the girls because I thought they were playing
another joke on me. One girl came over and asked me to dance, and
I didn't want to because I thought she was a man too, like in the
other place we went to. Then this buddy of mine told the girl what
happened at the other place. "I can prove it to you that I am not a
man," she said. "Come on, let's dance." So I danced with her. We
had a nice time there. We stayed there for a few hours, and then
I left.

We came to Guadalajara, and there we picked up some furniture, and then we fooled around in a couple of places. Then from
Guadalajara we went to Mexico City. And in Mexico City we went
to a place where we had to leave the furniture. We unloaded this
truck and got the furniture off, and then we went and rested for
one day.

The next day we went back to the truck and loaded it with more
furniture, and then we went to Saltillo to deliver this furniture. We
went to a lot of places in Saltillo. And there in Saltillo I met a nice girl,
a nice girl that belonged to a nice family. And I asked her if she
would like to be my girl there, and she said yes. And then every time
that we went to Monterrey I stopped in Saltillo and picked her up.
And I got too serious about her and even considered marrying her.
But I decided this girl was much too nice for me, because she came
from a rich family, and I had no money. That's why I decided to cut
her off.

I know how she felt, because she said, "I don't care if you have no money, because I have money and we can live very happy." But I don't like for a woman to support me. She was rich, and her father owned a couple of stores in Saltillo. I told her, "No, you are going to try and boss me around because you are the one with the money." "Well," she says, "if you don't want to, at least we can still be friends. When you come to Saltillo you can come and visit me, and if you decide we can talk it over again." "No," I said, "once I leave Saltillo I will never come back. I am even going to change jobs so I don't pass through Saltillo no more."

*   *   *

That's when I changed jobs, and I went with this boy to all these towns like Puebla, Veracruz, going all the way to the border of Guatemala. We went on that trip as salesmen. First we went to Puebla to try and sell like roosters made out of glass, or a clown made out of glass, and you can take the top off the clown and put wine inside. Then you can cover it again, and it just looks like a clown. We had different stuff, like a fish or an ashtray, all made out of glass.

We went to this town, Oaxaca, where they make a lot of good blankets. It is known for their good blankets. We went there to Oaxaca to sell some of this glass too. We stayed there two days. From there we went to the pyramids of Oaxaca. The pyramids are called Monte Albán. We also went there to try and sell some obsidian glass and obsidian stone that we took from San Juan. And we sold most of it in Oaxaca.

And then we went down into the state of Chiapas, almost to the Guatemala border. We wanted to go into Guatemala to a little town that I forget the name, so we went there to the border and asked the man if we could cross and he said, "You have to go and get permission." And we went, and they give us a little card, and they let us cross the border. We paid something like five dollars. That's sixty-two pesos. Five dollars for the little card to let us go through. We were in Guatemala for maybe three hours. We stayed around and visited the little shops around there.

We came back to Tepechitla, and we went to sell some glass, and then we went to get the train to Veracruz. See, we came from Teotihuacán on a bus to Mexico City. There in Mexico City we went to the bus station and got our ten big boxes, which weighed close to one ton, and we loaded them on this bus, and he charged us one hundred pesos for the freight of the boxes, to take them to Puebla. Then we were going to take all that merchandise to Veracruz on the train.

It was a long ride to Veracruz. It took about nineteen hours to get to Veracruz by train. And you know, in all those little towns there are a lot of women standing by the train selling tacos and tortillas, coffee. You don't have to get off the train to buy food. We buy everything, and when we got to the railroad station, right away we got one man to help us carry all the boxes.

We went to a hotel and rent a room and had all the merchandise in the room. Then we took a little merchandise out in a small box for samples and took them to the big stores in Veracruz to show them the samples. They would look them over, and they would say, "Well, I want so much of this, so much of that." And we sold quite a bit in Veracruz. And then from Veracruz we went to several more towns, and finally we bought a ticket home to Mexico City. And we had sold most of the merchandise.

*   *   *

In 1963 I moved from Mexico City to a town named Cholula near Puebla. I was living there with another aunt of mine. She's my mother's sister, and I lived there for a while. Her name was Carmelita Gonzales, and she got me a job with a leader. A leader is like a head, one of those that represents a union. He's the head man of the union. And I worked with him as a bodyguard. And then this leader, like he controls different factories, he put me to work in one of the factories he controlled. There I worked for about nine months, and I lived with my aunt and she gave me board and everything. I lived there, and I used to pay my aunt forty pesos for each week. Her three daughters used to wash my clothes and everything.

One day two of the daughters asked me to bring them to Mexico City for a visit. And I told them, "Well, I will save some money and then we will go." So I saved some money and then we come on the bus from Cholula to Mexico City, because this cousin of mine had a boyfriend that was living here in Mexico City. He's a mechanic.

So we came, and then we went around Chapultepec Park and we went to a movie. And right after the movie, me and my cousins, we couldn't go back to Cholula in that same day, so we stayed in a hotel.

And the boyfriend of my cousin, you know, he just said goodbye, and then he went. The next day we got up and her boyfriend was waiting. So he took us to the bus station, and then we drove back to Cholula again.

And then my aunt asked us, "Where did you stay in Mexico?" "Well," I told her, "we stayed in a hotel." And then my aunt says, "Did all three sleep in the same bed?" And I said, "Yes, we stayed all three of us in the same bed." And then my aunt says, "You didn't let them go by themselves?" With her boyfriend, you know. So I told her, "No, I didn't."

But my aunt is really one of these ladies that wants money all the time, and she doesn't care what happens to her daughters and things like that. When I was living there she used to tell her daughter, "Go ask your cousin for money." And my cousin would come and ask me for money. And I told my aunt, "It's not right you sending your daughter to ask me for money." And then my aunt used to come herself and ask me for money.

One day my aunt, she went out. I used to work nights, and I was sleeping and all of a sudden this first cousin of mine, she gets in bed with me. And I tell her, "Get out! You're my cousin and it's not right. And what would my aunt think!" And she says, "It's all right, a lot of cousins get married." And she wanted to get married with me. So I told her, "No, you get out, because one of these days I'm not going to feel sorry for you, and it will be bad for you. And you're just a young girl; you could find somebody to make you happy." And she said, "No, I love you," and all that, you know.

She was only nineteen, but she was doing that because her mother probably told her to take money from me. Because I was living there. And I tell her, "No, get out." I did this to her about four times. And then the last time she done that I couldn't resist, you know. And then she started going with me, this cousin of mine, for about six months.

Her mother would be sleeping in the next bed, and she used to crawl in the night and come and get into my bed all the time. And my aunt used to probably make believe that she was asleep, but my cousin used to sleep with her mother and get out of there and come over to me.

So finally I got tired of what my aunt was doing, sending her daughter to me, so I moved back to Mexico City. I got tired and said, "No, this is not right." I told her, "My aunt knows about it, and she doesn't get mad or nothing." So I went back to live with my aunt in Mexico City, Aunt Guadalupe. I left, and I didn't go back to see them for close to one year.

And then when I went back, I went back with my wife. And this cousin had a baby from another guy. It was about one year that I didn't go, and she had a baby there. And I asked her, "Whose is this baby?" And she told me, "Well, I don't know who's the father of the baby." She likes to flirt too much, you know. Even my wife said, "It's not good, because we went out, and right away she started talking to men." To a lot of guys. And my aunt doesn't get mad, but her sons get mad.

When I was living there in Cholula, my aunt used to get mad because I used to go visit my other cousins. They are married, and if I went to a movie with them, she used to get mad. She wanted me to all the time be with her and her daughters. Her husband died there while I was in Cholula. He died in the hospital of a heart attack.

So after that, in Mexico City I started selling *elotes,* you know, corn on the cob. You boil it, and then you sell it. With butter, chili pepper, like that. I didn't have no license so it was illegal for me to sell corn. But I used to sell it every day. So when I used to see the truck coming — they would pick you up and take your stand and load the corn and everything — we used to run, you know; we used to run.

So finally one day I couldn't run, so they took the whole thing away. They didn't arrest me, they just took the can of elotes. So I let them take it. I bought another can, because I used to pay to one cop, you know. I used to give him five pesos, ten pesos. But when the truck used to come, they didn't take no money, they take the can with the elotes. So finally I decided no, that's no good.

So I told my first cousin, "How come you don't give me a job in one of these hotels?" So I came to the San Juan Hotel and made an appointment and never heard anything from the San Juan Hotel. And then I met a guy and he told me, "How come you don't go to work in the tourist shops?" So that's when I started working at this kind of jobs, you know.

* * *

I came to work for the Tienda Azteca — not this Tienda Azteca here, but another Tienda Azteca. The same lady owns that one too. And I worked there for about nine months, and then that lady was so cranky I took off.

I went back to Mexico City, and I worked in another place, a turista place. In Mexico City they have a lot of stores for tourists. They have all kinds of stores, you know, silver stores, straw stores, and markets where they sell nothing but perfumes, French perfumes. Silver, gold, and everything for Americans that come from the States to buy.

I went to work in one of those stores, a jewelry store, where they sold gold rings and silver, sapphires, rubies, topaz, you know. I worked there for several months, and the tourists wasn't so good, so I changed jobs because I thought it would be better. I went to work in the glass factory in Mexico City. I worked there selling the glass, explaining how they make it and all that. I didn't like that job because it was too hot there. So I changed jobs again and went to work in another place in that same section, a place where they sell nothing but lacquer work. They made those wooden trays with all the colors, and I had to explain to the tourists how they made them. I worked there for a while too.

Then the season end, you know, the tourist season. And I couldn't make enough money, so I decided to change jobs. I went to work for a lady selling baskets and straw bags. The name of that store was Dos Hermanos. I was there for quite a while. And this lady was very nice to me. I would go visit her once in a while. And while I was working there I met a friend, a very close friend. His name was Sergio. We worked there together in the same store for a while, and then afterwards he changed jobs. He got another job close by, and we used to go to the movies, to the dances. And while we were working there was a girl there, and I started telling him to ask her to be his girl. Finally he decide to ask her, and she became his girl.

Right next to the place where we were working there was a girl named María. She was kind of old, she was around thirty-nine years old. And she had a son; her son was about fifteen years old. I kind of liked her, you know, but she was going around with another guy, and she told me she was very in love with him. So I couldn't . . . well, if she's very in love with him, I had better put her aside, out of mind, you know. I kind of liked her.

Finally I decided to come back to work for the Tienda Azteca. So I was there for a while, and then one day I had to go to my home town for the fiesta, which is on the second day of February every year. And I stayed for about one month there, and then I came back. And the lady there told me I didn't have no job. So I said, "That's OK." So I went to work in Mexico City for about one month.

And then this lady from this other Tienda Azteca here by the pyramids at Teotihuacán, she sent word with one guy to tell me to come and work for her. She offered me a higher salary, you know. She used to pay me 185 pesos, and then she went up to 200, to 275. Then afterwards, when I was going to leave, she said, "Don't go. I am going to pay you fifty pesos every day." So I kept on working for her, and that's when you came to us.

I was working there for nine months when you came there. We saw you there one day, and then you left. And the next day you came, and that's when you bought the blanket. When you bought the blanket, then the son of the lady who owns the Tienda Azteca told me I could show you around; you need somebody to show you around. And then I brought you to my house.

*   *   *

I met my wife at this Tienda Azteca by the pyramids. I met her here and you know, at first my wife, when I used to tell her to be my girlfriend, she would say, "Oh, you're crazy." She used to tell me that, and I would say, "You think I am crazy, but I am not crazy." I used to talk to her every day, and I used to invite her to the movies. She would tell me, "I could go to the movies with you, but I have to take my sister." And I used to tell her, "I am not taking your sister, I am taking you. What would your sister go for?" She says, "Well, you probably want to take me someplace else." "No, we would just go to the movies." So I told her, "Well, if you don't want to go, you can go someplace else." "Go to hell!" one time I told her. Finally I didn't pay any attention to her any more. I didn't say anything to her any more, even when she asked me some word in English or the price of something.

And then I saw her follow me around. And when we got off work, I used to tell her, "You go your way, I'll go mine." "No, I like to walk with you a little." And then we would go to San Juan. We used to stand there and talk, after work. Then I said, "You want to be my girlfriend?" And she says, "Yes."

With my wife, I never went around with her too much. I knew my wife for maybe one year before we got married, but she was not my girlfriend, actually just a working companion. She was only my girlfriend for eight days because on the ninth day I took her to Mexico City with me, and we stayed in a hotel there in Mexico City.

See, she had a cousin, and maybe she and her cousin made a plan. I still think that they had a plan, to get me. Because her cousin, one day he told me, "Let's go to Mexico City on the bus from San Juan." And it was late already, half-past seven. I told him OK, and we went to Mexico City, and then we went to a restaurant, and we ate some hot dogs and a banana split. Me and her and her cousin, all three of us.

And then I told the cousin, "Well, it's late, about half-past ten now, you better hurry up or you are going to be very late to get home." And then all of a sudden I was talking with her cousin, "You can go by yourself, she's going to stay here with me." And her cousin says, "I don't care as long as you give me something for my fare." So I give him five pesos. But I thought he was only kidding, you know. So then he got the five pesos, and we turned the corner, and all of a sudden we looked, and he was gone on the bus. Then I told her, "Now, if you like, I can take you home myself because he left." She says, "No, what is my father going to say if I go there with you?" "Well," I said, "then you can stay here with me." And we went in and rent a place in a hotel there.

And then we stayed there, and then the next day we got up, and we went to the floating gardens of Xochimilco all day. We stayed there all day on the grass, you know, talking. And we got a ride in a canoe, and had our photograph taken. And then we rent a little something you put over the grass, and you lay on it. And then pretty soon she said, "Well, we have to go to talk to my folks." And I was scared, scared to tell them, to talk to her folks. "Well," I says, "let's go!"

About four o'clock we got the bus for Mexico City, and then we got another bus to the pyramids. So we get off at San Juan and got a taxi to her house, and then we got out of the taxi, and her brother was there. I talked to the brother, and then we went in, and then I talked to her father and mother.

Her mother was mad, and she told me that her sons were there, and they were going to beat me up for taking her daughter. You know, I never done that, talked to the parents, so I was kind of scared. But I talked to them, and I said, "Well, I took your daughter, and I would like to get married with her." Her father was very under-standing, but her mother was really mad. Her father said, "Well, in view that you intend to marry with her, it's all right with me." But the mother, she was mad. And then one of the brothers said it was OK with him that I get married with her. He left. But the other brother was really mad; he didn't talk to me for about a week, and her mother was still mad. Her mother was the one that was worrying, and we talked and talked.

And the next day we went to work, and nobody knew that I had taken her with me, because we still went back to work like nothing happened. For two, three months I lived with her in her house. At first I used to stay with the two boys, the two brothers, you know. Sleep with them, all three in one bed. Then one day the brothers said, "Why don't you go sleep with Augustina?" My wife's name is Augustina. "You go sleep with Augustina." From then on I sleep every day with her. I sleep with her, and then finally we decide to get married.

So finally I told the lady at the Tienda Azteca that I was going to marry Augustina. And she told me, "No, it's no good for you to marry her." I said, "Why?" She says, "She's not your kind." She used to tell me things like that. While I was working there she used to tell me a lot of advice. She used to tell me, "I need a man to help me run this place." Because her husband is too old; he is good for nothing. But I never used to pay attention. She was around fifty-eight, sixty. I knew what she want, but I didn't pay any attention because I didn't like that. I didn't like her because I knew her daughters and her sons, and then there would be trouble, so that's why I never paid any attention to her. Then one day I asked her to let me go to San Juan to get married, and she got mad. She got mad, but anyway she gave me permission.

And my father-in-law and my mother-in-law went with me, and I got married there in San Juan. It cost me 125 pesos to get married, because I had to pay the witnesses. When I paid the witnesses off and everything, we came back to work.

We were married by law, not by church. They tell me that because I was not married by the church, I'm not married by the law of the church. And that's against our religion. But you know, I wouldn't like to. It seems like it is very hard to get married by the church. Because you have to learn every prayer. And I don't know how to pray. I don't pray very good, that's why it's kind of hard for me.

Then I was living with my mother-in-law, and we couldn't get along with my mother-in-law. We lived with her about two months, but I didn't get along with her, so we looked for this house which we are living in now. We rented the house, but we weren't living there because we didn't have any furniture in it. We just paid rent but we weren't living there. We were living with my mother-in-law.

Then my mother-in-law got mad, real mad, and we got out in the middle of the night, and we went to a neighbor's house for one night. So then on Saturday we went to Texcoco, and we bought a bed, on time. And we brought it in the house, and then we bought a kerosene stove, because we didn't have no money to buy one of those gas stoves. And then, little by little, we were buying stuff like a set of plates and cups and everything. Then we bought a closet where we put all our clothes in, and a cabinet for dishes.

*   *   *

Since the last time I was deported, I think I have been here in Mexico maybe four years. Before I never stayed that long. Back and forth, only two, three months here in Mexico and then going back to the States. But now I have stayed quite awhile. I would never go back again, unless I get, you know, permission or something. Before I never used to have a wife, maybe that's why I used to run back and forth. But now I have a wife. I never had a wife in the States, just girlfriends, that I used to go live with. You know, be there maybe six months, maybe a year, two years, like that. But I never had one wife that I would be married to her. I never felt like it. I didn't want to be tied down, I guess.

When my wife has a baby, I think my life would change. Because of the baby, you know. That would change my whole life, because I think I would try to set up a home, you know, a decent home like I never had myself. That's what I would like to do. That's why I am buying little by little furniture, because I would like to have a good house where people would go in and say you had a nice house. Maybe I couldn't buy it all at once, but I figure having a baby like that, it would change me. And I don't think I would go no place else. I think I would stay here.

And I am going to try to progress in any way that I can. If I think I can make more money at farming, I'll do that. If I think that's not going to work, maybe I'll try and put up a tourist store someplace. I know it takes money, but maybe I'll get money somewhere. I have been thinking about trying to get help from somebody from the States — just get the store and then pay him back. I don't know, I don't know. I would have to write. It would take at least five thousand dollars, about sixty thousand pesos. For a good business, you know. And I would have a place, maybe in Mexico City. I don't know where, but I will give it a try.

Mexico City is really a good place where you can set up one of those stores, because in Mexico City they attract an awful lot of tourist business. But I think I am better off in the country. You see, Mexico City is too much . . . the life is just too fast. If you stay in Mexico City, you want to go out all the time. You spend more money in the city than you do out here in the country. Life is easier here, more slow. Mexico City is too fast, just like being in New York. Everything going one way, everybody running. Same thing in Mexico City. Everybody is running around.

I would like to have a business. I know how to sell everything to the tourists, because by working in these places I have enough experience in selling and in how to buy even the merchandise. Because when I was at the Tienda Azteca even that lady used to ask me, "Is this the right price to pay for this?" And I used to tell her, "Well, I think it is this price." And she used to ask me, because I worked in a lot of places, you know.

If I would move to the border it would be nice too. But if I get a place in Mexico City I don't think I would move to the border, because the climate is better in Mexico City than in Mexicali. In Mexicali it is too hot. Sometimes it gets to 120, 130 degrees. Just like fire. Very hot. In Mexicali I have a lot of relatives. My grandfather owns a ranch. I would like to go there, maybe go work for him. No, not work for him! No, because when you work for your relatives, you never have a moment free. That's why I say I would like to have a place of my own. Since I have been here in Mexico the last few years, I have thought about that. That way you can be thinking about the future. Maybe later on you can get a bigger place. Maybe start with a small one, then a bigger one.

It's kind of hard to save enough money to start a business. Because you don't make enough money here. You only make fifty, sixty pesos a day, or maybe seventy-five at the most. Seventy-five pesos is about the most that a man makes around here in Mexico.

That's a salesman selling to the tourists. Any other man only makes about ten pesos, twelve, fifteen. Twenty-five is about the highest a man makes in a day. Look how lòng it would take you to save on twenty-five pesos a day! Yeah, I make more than that, but I mean, you know how high the food is in Mexico City. Look how much you spend. If you make twenty-five pesos, you spend it all on food and clothes. You never earn enough money to get a place. Here you can't get a loan like you can in the States. Here the only way you can get a loan is by having property. In the United States you can get a loan on your job. Here you don't have that kind of loan.

I'd like to own everything that I used to own in the States. Like a car, you know, and have a house. All good furniture inside. And then you can give the children education. That's why I would like to set up business or at least have a little money. And that way you can give your children education, so your children won't be running around like I did, you know.

And I want me and my wife to be together all the time. And then it won't happen like it happened to me. Like if I would ever leave my wife, then my children would be running around too. That's what I don't like, you know. I want to stay with my wife. I've already told her that I would never leave her. And sometimes I even joke with her. I tell her I'm going away, I'm going to leave her, and she starts crying, and right away I get her and tell her, "No, I just tell you that for fun."